Vocabulary for Key Stage 3 French

Editor
Philip Horsfall

Language Centre Publications

Vocabulary for Key Stage 3 French
Editor Philip Horsfall

First Published 1993
Reprinted 1994 & 1995
Design & typesetting by Image Plus Graphics Ltd.
Printed by The Vale Press Ltd.

ISBN 1 898583 02 1

HOW TO USE *VOCABULARY FOR KEY STAGE 3 FRENCH*

This book lists alphabetically all the words to be found currently in all the available French National Curriculum textbooks used to teach 11-14 year olds in this country. This is therefore the basic vocabulary to cover the areas of experience and the topics you are likely to meet in the course of studying French at school up to the age of 14.

What this book is *not* meant to be is a scholarly dictionary to rival the excellent comprehensive dictionaries on sale. Rather it aims to be a simple and first source of reference, an easy introduction to bilingual dictionary use without all the extra (and for Key Stage 3 unnecessary) baggage of a standard dictionary. For example it does not use abbreviations, phonetic script or any of the thousands of words not usually required at Key Stage 3. In order to give you confidence in looking up words and then using them, it is as user-friendly as possible; a first stepping-stone in easy-to-use format and clear lettering towards using the more academic dictionaries.

Unlike a standard dictionary, it is fully colour-coded for your ease of use. All headwords are listed alphabetically, with four main types of words in different colours. Any word printed in **green** is a verb (e.g. ***manger,*** or part of a verb (e.g. ***ai*** from ***avoir***) or the reflexive part of a reflexive verb (e.g. ***s'arrêter***). Before you can fully understand the meaning of a verb, you need to look at its tense and its endings. For example, ***manger*** is listed as "**to eat**", but in the context in which you find it, it may be ***il a mangé*** ("**he has eaten**") or ***mangez-vous?*** ("**do you eat?**"). Irregular forms of common verbs in the present tense are also listed alphabetically e.g. ***dit*** is listed as coming from ***dire*** and meaning "**says**".

Equally, if you look up the English word "**to eat**", you will find *manger*. But before you can use it, you will probably need to change the ending. The check list at the back of the book will help you find the correct ending to use.

Any word in **red** is a feminine noun (e.g. ***une fille*** = **girl**) whereas a word in blue is a masculine noun (e.g. ***un homme*** = **man**).

A **purple** word is an adjective (e.g. ***petit***) or a word which often acts like an adjective (e.g. ***construit***). These words describe nouns and have to change their endings accordingly, adding an extra "**e**" if feminine (e.g. ***une petite maison***) or an "**s**" if plural (e.g. *trois professeurs* ***sévères***). If the feminine form is not just a simple "**e**" on the end of the word, then the full form is given for easy reference (e.g. ***ancien/ancienne***).

Some words have more than one meaning, and you need to decide which is the suitable meaning from the passage in which the word occurs. For example, if the text is about newspapers and the word ***abonnement*** occurs, then the meaning is more likely to be "**subscription**" than "**season-ticket**".

The two headwords at the top of each page show the first and last word dealt with on that page, and the alphabet is printed on each page with the letter dealt with on that page in red, so that you can find the word you are looking for more easily.

There is a colour code reminder at the bottom of each page.

■ = masculine noun ■ = feminine noun ■ = verb ■ = adjective

The dictionary also includes at the back a useful check list of such areas as numbers, days of the week, months, times and seasons.

FRENCH-ENGLISH

A

il y a	there is; there are
à bas	down with
a *(from avoir)*	has
il/elle a *(from avoir)*	he/she has; he's/she's got
on a *(from avoir)*	we have; we've got
à 20 kilomètres	20 kilometres away
à bientôt	see you soon
à cinquante francs	costing fifty francs
à côté de	next to
à demain	see you tomorrow
à droite	to the right
à gauche	to the left
à haute voix	out loud
à l'aise	at ease
à l'étranger	abroad
à la campagne	in the country
à mon avis	in my opinion
à part	apart from; except
à peu près	more or less; approximately
à pied	on foot
à plat	flat (tyre)
à quatre kilomètres de...	four kilometres from...
à table	at table; to the table; dinner is served
un abattoir	slaughter-house
abdominal	(to do with the) stomach
un abonnement	season ticket; subscription
d' abord	first; at first; to begin with
un abri	shelter
un abricot	apricot
s' abriter	to shelter
absolument	absolutely
accepter	to accept; to take
un accès	access
accessible	accessible
un accident	accident
accompagné de	with; accompanied by
accompagner	to accompany
accompli	completed; carried out

■ = masculine noun ■ = feminine noun ■ = verb ■ = adjective

d' accord	OK; alright
être d' accord	to be in agreement
pas d' accord	not agreed
accorder les violons	to see eye to eye; to reach an agreement
un accueil	welcome; reception
un achat	purchase
faire des achats	to do some shopping
acheter	to buy
un acteur	actor
actif	active
active	active
une activité	activity
une actrice	actress
les actualités	news; current affairs
une addition	bill
additionner	to add up
une adhésion	membership
un adieu	farewell; goodbye
un adjectif	adjective
un ado (adolescent)	teenager
adorer	to love
une adresse	address
s' adresser à	to write to; to report to; to speak to (an adult)
l' aérobique	aerobics
un aéroglisseur	hovercraft
un aéroport	airport
les affaires	things; belongings
affectueuse	affectionate
affectueusement	yours affectionately (at end of a letter)
affectueux	affectionate
un affiche	poster; notice
afficher	to stick up; to put up
affreuse	awful; terrible
affreux	awful; terrible
africain	African
l' Afrique	Africa
un âge	age
âgé	aged; elderly
quel âge as-tu?	how old are you?
une agence	agency
une agence de publicité	advertising agency
une agence de voyages	travel agency
un agenda	diary

un agent de police	policeman
agile	agile
s' agir	to be about; to be a matter of
de quoi s' agit-il?	what's it all about?
une agitation	bustle; excitement
agréable	pleasant; nice
agressif	aggressive
agressive	aggressive
agricole	agricultural
j' ai (*from* avoir)	I have; I've got
j' ai ... ans	I am ... years old
une aide	help
aider	to help
aïe!	ouch! ow!
un aigle	eagle
une aiguille	hand (of a watch); needle
ailleurs	somewhere else
d' ailleurs	besides
aimable	kind; friendly
aimer	to like; to love
j' aimerais (*from* aimer)	I'd like
aimes-tu? (*from* aimer)	do you like?
aîné	older; elder
ainsi que	as well as; the same way as
l' air	air
en plein air	in the open (air)
ajouter	to add
un album de famille	family album
un alcool	alcohol
alcoolisé	alcoholic
Alger	Algiers
l' Algérie	Algeria
algérien	Algerian
algérienne	Algerian
un aliment	food; general food shop
j' allais (*from* aller)	I used to go
si on allait...? (*from* aller)	how about going to...?
je suis allé (*from* aller)	I went
alléché	tempted
une allée	way; aisle; avenue
l' Allemagne	Germany
en Allemagne	in/to Germany
allemand	German
l' allemand	German (the language)
aller	to go
s'en aller	to go away

aller à quelqu'un	to suit someone
aller au lit	to go to bed
un aller simple	single ticket
un aller-retour	return ticket
vous allez (*from* aller)	you're going; you go
allez tout droit	go straight on
allez!	go on! come on!
allez-y!	go ahead!
allô	hello (on the telephone)
allongé	stretched out
allons donc! (*from* aller)	that's silly!
allumé	lit
allumer	to light; to switch on
une allumette	match
alors	so; then; well
et alors?	so what?
l' alpinisme	climbing; mountaineering
un alpiniste	mountain-climber
une altitude	height
une amande	almond
un amateur d'histoire	history lover
une ambassade	embassy
l' ambiance	atmosphere
une âme	soul
amener	to take
amer	bitter
amère	bitter
américain	American
un ami	friend (male)
un petit ami	boy friend
amical	friendly
amicalement	yours; your friend (at end of a letter)
une amie	friend (female)
une petite amie	girl friend
une amitié	friendship
Amitiés	Love from; Best wishes (at end of a letter)
un amour	love
un film d' amour	love story (film)
amoureuse	in love
amoureux	in love
une ampoule	blister; bulb
amusant	fun; funny; amusing
amuse-toi!	have fun!
amuser	to amuse

■ = masculine noun ■ = feminine noun ■ = verb ■ = adjective

s' amuser	to enjoy oneself
un an	year
un ananas	pineapple
un ancêtre	ancestor
un anchois	anchovy
ancien	former; old
ancienne	former; old
un âne	donkey
une anémone de mer	sea anemone
un Anglais	Englishman
l' anglais	English (the language)
anglais	English
une Anglaise	Englishwoman
l' Angleterre	England
un animal	animal
des animaux	animals
animé	lively
un dessin animé	cartoon
un anneau	ring; circle
une année	year
une année scolaire	school year
un anniversaire	birthday
une annonce	announcement; advertisement
une annonce publicitaire	advertisement
annoncer	to announce
un anorak	anorak
antidérapant	non-slip
antillais	West Indian
les Antilles	West Indies
antiseptique	antiseptic
un antivol	padlock
anxieuse	anxious; worried
anxieux	anxious; worried
août	August
pas d' apartheid!	no apartheid!
un aperçu	glimpse; survey
l' apesanteur	weightlessness
un appareil	machine; telephone
un appareil électrique	electrical appliance
un appareil-photo	camera
une apparence	appearance
un appartement	flat; apartment
appartenir (à)	to belong (to)
cela m' appartient	that belongs to me
un appel	call; register
appeler	to call; to ring up

■ = masculine noun ■ = feminine noun ■ = verb ■ = adjective

s' appeler	to be called
comment t' appelles-tu?	what's your name?
bon appétit	enjoy your meal
un appétit	appetite
appliquer	to apply
apporter	to bring
une appréciation	assessment; appreciation
apprécier	to appreciate; to like
apprendre	to learn
j' apprends (*from* apprendre)	I learn
approcher	to get near
approprié	appropriate; suitable
approximativement	roughly
appuyer	to press
après	after; at the end of
un après-midi	afternoon
un aquarium	aquarium
un Arabe	Arab
arabe	Arabian
une araignée	spider
un arbre	tree
un arbre généalogique	family tree
un arc	bow
le tir à l' arc	archery
un arc-en-ciel	rainbow
une arche	arch; ark
l' archéologie	archaeology
l' argent	money; silver
l' argent de poche	pocket money
une armée	army
une armoire	wardrobe
l' arnica	arnica (a herbal medicine)
un mandat d'arrestation	arrest warrant
un arrêt	stop
un arrêt d'autobus	bus stop
arrêter	to stop; to arrest
s' arrêter	to stop
en arrière	in/at the back; backwards
arrière droit	right back (football)
une arrière grand-mère	great grandmother
un arrière grand-père	great grandfather
une arrivée	arrival
arriver	to arrive; to come
arriver à quelqu'un	to happen to somebody
arrogant	arrogant; conceited
arrondir	to round up

un arrondissement	district of Paris
arroser	to water; to spray
l' art dramatique	drama
un artichaut	artichoke
un article	article; item
l' artisanat	arts and crafts
un artiste	performer; star; artist
une artiste	performer; star; artist
tu as (*from* avoir)	you have; you've got
un as de pique	ace of spades
un ascenseur	lift; elevator
l' Asie	Asia
un aspirateur	vacuum cleaner
une aspirine	aspirin
s' asseoir	to sit down
asseyez-vous! (*from* *s'*asseoir)	sit down!
assez	quite; enough
assez de	enough
assieds-toi (*from* *s'*asseoir)	sit down
une assiette	plate
une assiette anglaise	plate of cold cooked meats
assis	sitting down; seated
une association sportive	sports association/club
astrologique	astrological
un astrologue	astrologer
un astronef	spacecraft
l' astuce	wit; cleverness
un atelier	workshop
un athlète	athlete
l' athlétisme	athletics
faire de l' athlétisme	to do athletics
atlantique	Atlantic
un atlas	atlas
une atmosphère	atmosphere
un atout	asset; great advantage
attacher	to fasten; to fix
attaquer	to attack
attendre	to wait; to wait for
attention!	watch out! careful!
attentivement	carefully; attentively
atterrir	to land
attirer	to attract
un parc d' attractions	theme park
attraper	to catch
au	at; in; to (with a masculine word)

au lieu de	instead of
au revoir	goodbye
au secours!	help!
au téléphone	on the telephone
au troisième top	at the third stroke
au-dessus	above
une auberge	inn
une auberge de jeunesse	youth hostel
une aubergine	aubergine
aucun	no; not any
une audace	daring
audacieuse	bold
audacieux	bold
des auditeurs	listeners
aujourd'hui	today
il y aurait (*from* avoir)	there would be; it would have
aussi	too; also
aussi ... que	as ... as
aussitôt	straightaway
l' Australie	Australia
australien	Australian
australienne	Australian
un auteur	author
authentique	real; authentic
un autobus	bus
un autocollant	sticker
un autographe	autograph
l' automne	autumn
en automne	in autumn
un autoportrait	self-portrait
autoritaire	bossy; authoritarian
une autoroute	motorway
autour	around
autour de la maison	around the house
autre	other; different
quelqu'un d'autre	someone else
autrefois	in days gone by
autrement	otherwise; differently
les autres	the others
l' Autriche	Austria
une autruche	ostrich
aux	in the; to the; at the (with a plural word)
j' avais (*from* avoir)	I had
avaler	to swallow
d' avance	in advance

■ = masculine noun ■ = feminine noun ■ = verb ■ = adjective

en avance	in advance; early
pays avancé	developed country
avancer	to put forward; to go forward
avant	before
avant de partir	before leaving
un avantage	advantage
avec	with
un avenir	future
à l' avenir	in (the) future
une aventure	adventure
un film d' aventure	adventure film
aventurier	adventurous
aventurière	adventurous
une avenue	avenue
aveugle	blind
vous avez (*from* avoir)	you have; you've got
un avion	aeroplane
un avis	opinion
à mon avis	in my opinion
avoir	to have
avoir besoin de	to need
avoir chaud	to be hot
avoir de la chance	to be lucky
avoir de la fièvre	to have a temperature
avoir faim	to be hungry
avoir froid	to be cold
avoir l'air	to seem
avoir lieu	to take place
avoir mal à la tête	to have a headache
avoir peur	to be afraid
avoir soif	to be thirsty
avoir un supermoral	to have a lot of pluck
nous avons (*from* avoir)	we have; we've got
avril	April
en avril	in April
ayant (*from* avoir)	having

B

le babyfoot	table football
le badminton	badminton
des bagages	luggage
une bague	ring
une baguette	French loaf
une baie	bay
se baigner	to have a swim
une baignoire	bath tub
bâiller	to yawn
un bain	bath
un bain moussant	bubble bath
baisser	to lower
un bal	dance
une balade	walk
faire une balade	to go for a walk/stroll
une balade à bicyclette	bicycle ride
se balader	to go for a walk
un baladeur	walkman
un balai	broom
Balance	Libra
une balance	scales
une balançoire	swing; see-saw
balayer	to sweep
un balcon	balcony
Bâle	Basle
une baleine	whale
une balle	ball (small)
des ballerines	flat pumps
un ballon	ball (large); balloon
un ballon de foot	football
le bambou	bamboo
une banane	banana
un banc	bench
une bande	group; tape
une bande adhésive	stick-on strip
une bande dessinée	comic strip
une banlieue	suburb
en banlieue	in the suburbs
une banque	bank
un banquier	banker
une banquise	ice field
c'est barbant	it's boring
un barbare	Barbarian

■ = masculine noun ■ = feminine noun ■ = verb ■ = adjective

c'est la barbe	it's a bore
une barbe	beard
quelle barbe!	what a bore!
un barbecue	barbecue
un barman	barman
une barque	small boat
une barre	bar
une barre aux céréales	muesli bar
une barre chocolatée	chocolate bar
des barreaux	bars; rails
barrer	to cross out
une barrière	gate
en bas	downstairs
bas	down
bas	low
en bas de	at the bottom of
basculer	to wobble; to tip up
le basilic	basil
le basket	basketball
des baskets	trainers
un basketteur	basketball player
basse	low
une basse	bass (guitar)
une bataille	battle
un bateau	boat
un bateau-mouche	river boat in Paris for tourists
un bâtiment	building
un bâton de colle	stick of glue
la batterie	percussion; drums
un batteur	drummer
battre	to beat
battre les cartes	to shuffle cards
battre les records	to break the records
bavard	talkative
bavarder	to chat
une B.D.	comic
beau	handsome; beautiful
faire beau	to be fine weather
un beau-père	step-father
beaucoup	a lot; very much; many
les beaux-arts	fine arts
un bébé	baby
un bec	beak
une flûte à bec	recorder
une bêche	spade
belge	Belgian

■ = masculine noun ■ = feminine noun ■ = verb ■ = adjective

la Belgique	Belgium
Bélier	Aries
belle	beautiful; lovely
une belle-mère	stepmother
ben...	well...
les béquilles	crutches
une berge	river bank
un berger allemand	alsatian dog
un berlingot	boiled sweet
un bermuda	Bermuda shorts
un besoin	need
avoir besoin de	to need
bête	stupid
une bête	beast
une bêtise	mistake; silliness
une betterave	beetroot
beurk!	yuk!
le beurre	butter
beurré	buttered
une bibliothèque	library; bookcase
un bic	biro; ballpoint pen
une bicyclette	bicycle
un bidon	container
c'est bidon	it's boring; it's a load of rubbish
bien	good; well
et bien	well
ou bien	or else
bien sûr	of course
bientôt	soon
à bientôt	see you soon
bienvenu	welcome
bienvenue à vous	welcome!
une bière	beer
un bifteck	beefsteak
bilingue	bilingual
le billard américain	pool
une bille	marble
un billet	ticket; banknote
un billet de banque	bank note
la biologie	biology
une biscotte	French toast
un biscuit	biscuit
une bise	kiss
grosses bises	hugs and kisses (at end of a letter)

un bisou	kiss
bizarre	strange
une blague	joke
blanc	white
un blanc	gap (in a text)
blanche	white
le blé	wheat; corn
un bled perdu	godforsaken hole
blessé	injured; hurt
bleu	blue
un bleu	bruise
bleu marine ***(never changes)***	navy blue
un bloc	notebook
un bloc sanitaire	washing facilities
blond	blond; fair
bloquer	to block
une blouse	overall
un blouson	casual jacket
un blue-jeans	jeans
un bobo	pain; sore
un bocal	jar
un body	leotard
un boeuf	ox; beef
bof!	huh! who cares?
boire	to drink
un bois	wood
en bois	made of wood
je bois (***from*** boire)	I drink
une boisson	drink
une boisson chaude	hot drink
une boisson froide	cold drink
il/elle boit (***from*** boire)	he/she drinks
une boîte	box; tin; nightclub
une boîte à couture	sewing box
un bol	bowl
une bombe	spray
bon	good; correct
un bon	coupon
bon anniversaire	happy birthday
bon appétit	enjoy your meal!
bon courage!	good luck!
un bon de commande	order form
bon séjour!	enjoy your stay!
bon voyage!	have a good journey!
ah bon?	oh yes?
un bonbon	sweet

■ = masculine noun ■ = feminine noun ■ = verb ■ = adjective

une bonbonne	canister; demijohn
un bonhomme	chap; bloke; man
un bonhomme de neige	snowman
bonjour	hello
bonne	good; correct
bonne chance	good luck
bonne fête!	happy name day! (from saint's days)
de bonne heure	early
bonne nuit	good night
un bonnet	cap
bonsoir	good evening
à bord	aboard
un bord	edge
au bord de	on the edge of; next to
au bord de la mer	by the sea
bordeaux (*never changes*)	dark red; maroon
une bosse	hump; bump; lump
des bottes	boots
un bouc	billy-goat
une bouche	mouth
un boucher	butcher
une bouchère	butcher
une boucherie	butcher's
un bouchon	top; cork (of bottle; etc)
bouclé	curly
une boucle d'oreille	earring
boucler	to fasten
une boue	mud
bouffer	to eat; to gobble up
bouger	to move
une bougie	candle
(faire) bouillir	to boil
une bouillotte	hot water bottle
un boulanger	baker
une boulangerie	baker's
une boule	bowling ball; crystal ball
jouer aux boules	to play bowls
un boulevard	wide street (often with trees)
un boulot	work
une boum	party; disco
un bouquet	bunch
une boussole	compass
un bout	end
au bout (de)	at the end (of)
une bouteille	bottle

une boutique	shop
un bouton	spot; button
la boxe	boxing
branché	'with-it'
un bras	arm
un brassard	armband
bravo	well done; congratulations
une brebis	ewe
la Bretagne	Brittany
des bretelles	braces
breton	from Brittany
bretonne	from Brittany
un brevet	certificate
le bricolage	D.I.Y.; odd jobs
brillant	shining
briller	to shine
une brioche	sort of bun
britannique	British
une broche	brooch
une brochette	kebab
une brochure	brochure
le bronzage	sunbathing
bronzé	tanned
bronzer	to sunbathe
une brosse	brush
une brosse à cheveux	hairbrush
une brosse à dents	toothbrush
brosser	to brush
se brosser	to brush
le brouillard	fog
faire du brouillard	to be foggy
brouillé	jumbled
un bruit	noise
le bruitage	sound effects
brûler	to burn
une brute	brute; bully
un brute	brute; bully
Bruxelles	Brussels
bruyant	noisy
j'ai bu (*from* boire)	I've drunk
un buffet	sideboard; snackbar
une bulle	bubble
un bulletin	bulletin; report
un bulletin scolaire	school report
un bulletin trimestriel	termly school report
un bulletin-réponse	answer-form

■ = masculine noun ■ = feminine noun ■ = verb ■ = adjective

un bureau	desk; office; study
un bureau de poste	post office
un bureau de renseignements	information office
un bureau du principal	head's office
une burette	oil can
un but	purpose; goal
une buvette	refreshment bar

C

c'	it (before a vowel)
c'est (*from* être)	this is; it is
c'est qui?	who is it?
c'est tout	that's all
c'est-à-dire	that is to say; I mean
ça	this; that
ça alors!	you don't say! good grief!
ça bouge!	things are really moving!
ça dépend	it depends
ça fait mal	it hurts
ça ne fait rien	that doesn't matter
ça ne va pas	something's wrong; that won't do
ça suffit!	that's enough!
ça te dit...?	do you fancy...?
ça va	things are OK; that's all right; that's enough; I'm fine
ça va mal	things are going badly
ça va mieux?	are you better?
ça va sans dire	that goes without saying
ça va?	how are you?
ça y est	that's it; we've done it
une cabane	hut
une cabane à lapins	rabbit hutch
une cabine	cabin; booth
une cabine d'essayage	dressing room
une cabine téléphonique	telephone kiosk
un cabinet médical	doctor's surgery
un câble	cable
un cacao	cocoa
caché	hidden
un cache-nez	scarf
cacher	to hide
un cadeau	present; gift
des cadeaux	presents; gifts
un cadre	box; square space; frame
un cafard	cockroach
j'ai le cafard	I'm fed up
un café	café; coffee
un café-crème	white coffee
une cage	cage
un cahier	exercise book
un cahier d'appel	register

■ = masculine noun ■ = feminine noun ■ = verb ■ = adjective

un cahier de brouillon	rough book
le Caire	Cairo
une caisse	till; check-out; cash-desk
un caissier	cashier
une caissière	cashier
un calcul	sum; calculation
une calculatrice	calculator
calculer	to calculate; to work out
un caleçon cycliste	cycling shorts
un calendrier	calender
un calepin	notebook
un calmar	squid
calme	calm; quiet
calme-toi!	calm down!
calmez-vous!	calm down!
un camarade	friend
une camarade	friend
cambrioler	to burgle
un camembert	camembert cheese
un caméraman	cameraman
le Cameroun	The Cameroons
un camion	lorry
une camionnette	van
une campagne	countryside
à la campagne	in the countryside
en pleine campagne	deep in the countryside
camper	to camp
un camping	campsite
le Canada	Canada
canadien	Canadian
canadienne	Canadian
un canapé	settee; sofa
un canard	duck
un candidat	candidate
une candidate	candidate
un caniche	poodle
un canif	penknife
une canne	stick
une canne à pêche	fishing rod
du canoë	canoeing
un canoë-kayak	canoe
un canot	canoe
le canotage	canoeing
une cantine	canteen
(en) caoutchouc	(made of) rubber
une cape	cloak; cape

un capitaine	captain
une capitale	capital city
car	because; for
un car	coach
en car	by bus/coach
un caractère	character
caraïbe	Caribbean
un cardigan	cardigan
caresser	to stroke
une caricature	caricature
un carnet	report; book; book of tickets (for Paris underground)
un carnet de timbres	book of stamps
un carnival	carnival
une carotte	carrot
un carré	square
carré	square
à carreaux	checked; chequered
un carrefour	crossroads
un cartable	school bag
une carte	card; map; menu
une carte bleue	credit card (Visa)
une carte d'adhérent	membership card
une carte d'identité	identity card
une carte d'invitation	an invitation
une carte postale	postcard
en cas de	in case of
une cascade	waterfall
une case	space; square; box; grid
un casque	helmet; headphones
une casquette	cap
cassé	broken
un casse-cou	daredevil
un casse-croûte	snack
un casse-pieds	nuisance; pain in the neck
un casse-tête	brain teaser
casser	to break
une casserole	saucepan
une cassette	cassette
une cassette-vidéo	video cassette
un cassis	blackcurrant
une castagnette	castanet
un castor	beaver
un catadioptre	reflector
une catastrophe	catastrophe; disaster
catastrophique	catastrophic; disastrous

■ = masculine noun ■ = feminine noun ■ = verb ■ = adjective

le catch	wrestling
le catéchisme	catechism (religious instruction)
une catégorie	category
une cathédrale	cathedral
un cauchemar	nightmare
à cause de	because of
une caution	deposit
une cave	cellar
le C.D.I. (centre de documentation et d'information)	school resource centre
la C.E.	the EC (European Community)
ce	this
ce que	what
en ce qui concerne...	as far as...is concerned
ceci	this
céder	to give in
une ceinture	belt
une ceinture de sauvetage	safety belt
cela	that
célèbre	famous
celle(s)-ci	this one (these)
celle(s)-là	that one (those)
celles	the ones
celui-ci	this one
celui-là	that one
Cendrillon	Cinderella
cent	hundred
des centaines de...	hundreds of...
un centième	100th
un centime	100th of a franc; one centime
un centimètre	centimetre
un centre	centre
un centre commercial	shopping centre
un centre de loisirs	leisure centre
un centre sportif	sports centre
un centre-ville	town centre
un cerceau	ring; hoop
un cercle	circle
cercler	to circle
une céréale	cereal
une cérémonie	ceremony
un cerf-volant	kite
une cerise	cherry
certains	some; some people

un cerveau	brain
un C.E.S	secondary school; comprehensive school
ces	these; those
cesser	to stop; to cease
cet	this (in front of a masculine noun beginning with a vowel)
cette	this; that (in front of a feminine noun)
ceux	those (masculine)
chacun	everybody; each one; every one
un chahut	uproar
une chaîne	chain
une chaîne de montagnes	mountain range
une chaîne de télévision	television channel
une chaîne hi-fi	hi-fi system
une chaîne stéréo	stereo
la chair de poule	goose pimples
avoir la chair de poule	to have goose pimples
une chaise	chair
la chaleur	heat
une chambre	bedroom
un chameau	camel
un champ	field
le champagne	champagne
un champignon	mushroom
un champion	champion
un championnat	championship
une championne	champion
une chance	luck
bonne chance	good luck
changer	to change
changer de place	to change seats
une chanson	song
le chant	singing
chanter	to sing
un chanteur	singer
une chanteuse	singer
un chantier	building site; roadworks
la Chantilly	whipped cream
un chapeau	hat
un chapeau melon	bowler hat
chaque	each; every
chaque fois	each time
un char	float; tank

■ = masculine noun ■ = feminine noun ■ = verb ■ = adjective

du char à voile	sand-yachting
une charcuterie	pork butcher's; delicatessen
de la charcuterie	cooked cold meat
charger	to load up
un chariot	trolley
une charité	charity
charmant	charming; lovely
une chasse	hunting; hunt
chasser	to hunt; to chase
un chat	cat
châtain (***never changes***)	chestnut brown; auburn
un château	castle; stately home
un chaton	kitten
une chatte	female cat
chaud	hot; warm
il fait chaud	it's hot
j'ai chaud	I'm hot
le chauffage central	central heating
chauffer	to heat
un chauffeur	driver
un chauffeur de taxi	taxi driver
une chaumière	cottage
une chaussette	sock
un chausson	turnover (pie or pastry)
des chaussons	slippers; ballet shoes
une chaussure	shoe
des chaussures à crampons	boots with studs
une chauve-souris	bat
un chef	chief
en chef	in chief
un chef d'oeuvre	masterpiece
un chef de cuisine	cook
un chemin	way
un chemin de fer	railway
une cheminée	fireplace; chimney
une chemise	shirt
une chemise de nuit	nightdress
un chemisier	blouse
une chenille	caterpillar
un chèque	cheque
un chèque de voyage	traveller's cheque
un chéquier	cheque book
cher	dear; expensive
chercher	to look for; to get
chère	dear; expensive
un chéri	darling

■ = masculine noun ■ = feminine noun ■ = verb ■ = adjective

une chérie	darling
un cheval	horse
un chevalier	knight
des chevaux	horses
une table de chevet	bedside table
les cheveux	hair
une cheville	ankle
une chèvre	goat
chez	at/to someone's home
chez elle	at/to her house
chez le médecin	to/at the doctor's
chez moi	at/to my house
chez nous	at our house
chez toi	at your place
chez vous	at your house
chic	smart; great
un chien	dog
une chienne	female dog; bitch
un chiffon	duster; rag; cloth
un chiffre	number
des chiffres romains	Roman numerals
la chimie	chemistry
chimique	chemical
un chimiste	chemist
un chimpanzé	chimpanzee
la Chine	China
chinois	Chinese
un chiot	puppy
des chips	crisps
un chirurgien	surgeon
un choc	shock
un chocolat	chocolate; drinking chocolate
choisi	chosen
choisir	to choose
un choix	choice
le chômage	unemployment
au chômage	unemployed
chômeur	unemployed
chômeuse	unemployed
choquant	shocking
une chorale	choir
une chose	thing
un chou	cabbage; darling
un chou-fleur	cauliflower
un chouchou	teacher's pet
chouette	great; nice; super

■ = masculine noun ■ = feminine noun ■ = verb ■ = adjective

une chouette	owl
se chronométrer	to time oneself
un chrysanthème	chrysanthemum
chut!	sshh! quiet!
une chute	waterfall; fall
Chypre	Cyprus
ci-contre	opposite
ci-dessous	below; underneath
ci-dessus	above
un cidre	cider
un ciel	sky
une cigarette	cigarette
un ciné	cinema
un cinéaste	film maker
un cinéma	cinema
cinq	five
cinquante	fifty
cinquième	fifth
je suis en cinquième	I'm in year 8
un circuit	track; route
un circuit de voitures	car track
la circulation	traffic
circuler	to go; to move
cirer	to polish
un cirque	circus
des ciseaux	scissors
une citadelle	fortress
une cité	city; estate; hall of residence
un citoyen	citizen
un citron	lemon
un citron pressé	squeezed lemon drink
une citronnade	still lemonade; lemon squash
clair	light
claqué	worn out; bushed
claquer des doigts	to snap one's fingers
faire des claquettes	to tap dance
une clarinette	clarinet
une classe	classroom; class
en classe	in the classroom; at school
classique	classical
un clavier	keyboard
une clé	key
une clef	key
un client	client; customer
une cliente	client; customer
une clientèle	customers

■ = masculine noun ■ = feminine noun ■ = verb ■ = adjective

un climat	climate
une climatisation	air-conditioning
un clochard	tramp
une cloche	bell
une clochette	small bell
un clou du spectacle	high point of the show
un club de judo	judo club
un club des jeunes	youth club
un cobaye	guinea pig
un Coca; Coca-Cola	Coca-Cola
cocher	to tick
un cochon	pig
un cochon d'Inde	guinea pig
une noix de coco	coconut
un cocotier	coconut tree
un code de la route	highway code
un coeur	heart
un coiffeur	hairdresser
une coiffeuse	hairdresser
une coiffure	hairstyle
un coin	corner; neighbourhood
en colère	angry
coléreuse	irritable; bad-tempered
coléreux	irritable; bad-tempered
en colimaçon	spiral
un collant	pair of tights
une collection	collection
collectionner	to collect
un collège	secondary school
un collègue	colleague
coller	to stick
une colline	hill
une colonie de vacances	summer camp
une colonne	column
colorier	to colour in
combien de?	how much?; how many?
une combinaison de ski	ski suit
le comble	worst thing
une comédie musicale	musical
un comédien	actor
une comédienne	actress
comique	comic
un commandant	commander
une commande	order
comme	as; like
comme ci comme ça	neither good nor bad; so-so

■ = masculine noun ■ = feminine noun ■ = verb ■ = adjective

commencer	to start; to begin
comment	how; what; what like
c'est comment?	what's it like?
comment allez-vous?	how are you?
comment ça va?	how are you?
comment est...?	what is...like?
comment s'appelle-t-il?	what is he called?
comment t'appelles-tu?	what's your name
comment tu trouves...?	what do you think of...?
un commentaire	commentary
un commerçant	shop keeper
un commissariat	police station
un commissariat de police	police station
une commode	chest of drawers
commode	convenient
en commun	public
la Communauté Économique Européenne	European Economic Community
communiquer	to communicate
une compagnie	company
une comparaison	comparison
comparer à	to compare with
un compartiment	compartment
complet	full; full up
complète	full; full up
complètement	completely
complexe	complicated
compliqué	complicated
comportant	including; covering
composé de	made of
un compositeur	composer
composter	to punch a ticket; to stamp
un composteur	ticket-punch; stamp
une compote de pommes	stewed apple; apple sauce
comprendre	to understand
une compresse	dressing; compress
un comprimé	pill; tablet
compris	included
tu as compris? (*from* comprendre)	have you understood?
compter	to count; to add up
une comptine	rhyme
un comptoir	(shop) counter
un comte	count
un concert	concert
un concierge	caretaker

■ = masculine noun ■ = feminine noun ■ = verb ■ = adjective

une concierge	caretaker
un concombre	cucumber
un concours	competition
un concours de composition	writing competition
un concours de vitessse	speed contest
un concurrent	competitor
une concurrente	competitor
condamner	to condemn
une condition	condition
un conducteur	driver
conduire	to drive
une confiance	confidence
confiant	confident
confier	to confide in
une confiserie	sweet shop
une confiture	jam
une confiture d'orange	marmalade
confortable	comfortable
confus	confused; embarrassed
un congé	holiday
un congélateur	deep freeze
je/tu connais (*from* connaître)	I/you know
une connaissance	knowledge
faire la connaissance de	to meet; to get to know
connaître	to know
connu (*from* connaître)	known
une conquête	conquest
consacré	devoted
consciencieuse	conscientious
consciencieux	conscientious
un conseil	piece of advice
un Conseil Municipal des Jeunes	Junior Council
un conseiller d'éducation	year tutor
un conservatoire	music academy
une consigne	left lugguge office
une consigne automatique	left luggage locker
consommer	to consume
construire	to build
construit en...	built in...
consulter	to consult
contenir	to contain
content	pleased; happy
le contenu	contents
un continent	continent
continuellement	continuously
continuer	to continue

■ = masculine noun ■ = feminine noun ■ = verb ■ = adjective

se contracter	to tense; to tighten
au contraire	on the contrary
un contraire	opposite
contre	against; versus
par contre	on the other hand
une contrebasse	double bass
contribuer	to contribute
un contrôle	check-point; test
un contrôleur	ticket collector
une conversation	conversation
en pleine conversation	deep in conversation
un copain	friend; pal
une copie	copy
copier	to copy
une copine	friend; pal
un coq	cockerel
le coq au vin	chicken cooked in wine
une coque	cockle
un coquillage	shell
une coquille d'un escargot	snail shell
un cor	horn (musical instrument)
un corbeau	crow
une corbeille	bin; basket
une corde	string; rope; skipping rope
une corne	horn (of animal)
un cornichon	gherkin
un corps	body
une correspondance	train connection
un correspondant	penfriend
correspondant	matching; corresponding
une correspondante	penfriend
correspondre	to write to someone; to link; to match
corriger	to correct
la Corse	Corsica
un costume	costume; suit
une côte	coast; chop; rib
la Côte d'Azur	Riviera
la Côte d'Ivoire	Ivory Coast
un côté	side
d'un côté	on one side
à côté de	next to; beside
une côtelette	chop; cutlet
une cotisation	subscription
le coton	cotton
le coton hydrophile	cotton wool

■ = masculine noun ■ = feminine noun ■ = verb ■ = adjective

un cou	neck
une couche d'ozone	ozone layer
le soleil se couche	the sun sets
se coucher	to go to bed
une couchette	bunk for sleeping
coucou!	hi! (to a friend)
un coude	elbow
coudre	to sew
une couleur	colour
un couloir	corridor
un coup	blow
un coup de foudre	love at first sight
un coup de main	helping hand
un coup de soleil	sunstroke; sunburn
un coup de téléphone	phone call
un coupable	culprit
une coupe	cup; trophy
coupé	cut
couper	to cut
se couper	to cut oneself
une cour	playground
courageuse	brave
courageux	brave
un courant	current
en courant	running
un coureur	runner
courir	to run; to race
une couronne	crown
le courrier	letters; mail; post
le courrier du coeur	problem page
un cours	class; lesson
un cours de change	an exchange rate
une course	race
des courses	shopping
faire des courses	to go shopping
un coursier	dispatch rider
court	short
un court	court
il/elle court (*from* courir)	he/she runs
un courtisan	courtier
couru (*from* courir)	run
un cousin	cousin
une cousine	cousin
un coussin	cushion
un couteau	knife
coûter	to cost

■ = masculine noun ■ = feminine noun ■ = verb ■ = adjective

coûteuse	costly; expensive
coûteux	costly; expensive
des coutumes	customs; habits
la couture	sewing
un couvercle	cover; lid
couvert	covered
un couvert	place setting
mettre le couvert	to set the table
une couverture	blanket
un couvre-lit	bedspread
couvrir	to cover
un cracheur de feu	fire-eater
un crâne	skull
un crapaud	toad
craquer pour	to be desperate for
une cravate	tie
un crayon	pencil
créé	created
créer	to create
un crème	coffee with milk
une crème	cream
une crème solaire	sun cream
une crèmerie	dairy
une crêpe	pancake
une crêperie	pancake restaurant; pancake stall
creuse	empty; hollow
creusé	dug out
creux	empty; hollow
une crevaison	puncture
crevé	worn out; tired out
une crevette	shrimp
crier	to shout
la Crimée	Crimea
croire	to believe; to think so
je crois (*from* croire)	I think; I believe
des mots croisés	crossword
une croisière	cruise
une croissance	growth
un croissant	croissant
une croix	cross
la Croix Rouge	Red Cross
un croque-monsieur	toasted sandwich with ham and cheese
une crosse	hockey stick
la crotte	droppings; dung; rubbish

■ = masculine noun ■ = feminine noun ■ = verb ■ = adjective

des crudités	raw vegetable starter
cruel	cruel
cruelle	cruel
cueillir	to pick
un cui-cui	cooing
une cuiller	spoon
une cuillère	spoon
une cuillère à soupe	dessert spoon
une cuillerée	spoonful
le cuir	leather
en cuir	made of leather
cuire	to cook
une cuisine	kitchen; cooking
faire la cuisine	to cook
un cuisinier	cook
une cuisinière	cooker
une cuisse	thigh
une cuisse de grenouille	frog's leg
une culotte	pants
cultiver	to grow
un curé	priest
curieuse	curious
curieux	curious
une curiosité	sight; item of interest
un cycle d'eau	water cycle
le cyclisme	cycling
faire du cyclisme	to go cycling
un cycliste	bike-rider
un cyprès	cypress tree

D

d'	(short for de)
d'abord	first; at first
d'accord	alright; OK
le daim	suede
une dame	lady
une dame de trèfle	queen of clubs
les dames	ladies (toilet); draughts
la dance classique	ballet
le Danemark	Denmark
dangereuse	dangerous
dangereux	dangerous
danois	Danish
dans	in; into
la danse	dancing
danser	to dance
un danseur	dancer
une danseuse	dancer
une date	date
une date de naissance	date of birth
un dauphin	dolphin
de	of; from; any
un dé	dice
un débardeur	tank-top
débarquer	to unload; to disembark
débarrasser la table	to clear the table
débile	feeble; useless
debout	standing
débrouiller	to unscramble
se débrouiller	to manage; to cope
un début	beginning
au début (de)	at the beginning (of)
un décalage horaire	time difference
décembre	December
les déchets	rubbish
déchiffrer	to decipher; to decode
déchirer	to tear; to rip up
décidément	definitely; certainly
se décider à	to make one's mind up to
décider de	to decide to
déclarer	to declare
un décollage	take-off (of an aeroplane)
décolleté	low-necked
décontracté	relaxed

■ = masculine noun ■ = feminine noun ■ = verb ■ = adjective

décoré	decorated
découper	to cut out; to cut up
découragé	discouraged
un découragement	discouragement
une découverte	discovery
découvrir	to discover
décrire	to describe
ils se décrivent (*from* décrire)	they are describing themselves
dedans	inside; in it
défaire	to undo; to unpack
un défaut	fault; failing
défavorisé	underprivileged
défendre	to defend
une défense	tusk
défense de...	it's forbidden/not allowed to...
un défilé	procession
un défilé de mode	fashion show
un dégât	damage
dégonfler	to let down; deflate
un degré	degree
se déguiser	to disguise oneself; to dress up
une dégustation	tasting
déguster	to taste; to sample; to enjoy
(au) dehors	outside
déjà	already
un déjeuner	lunch; midday meal
un petit déjeuner	breakfast
déjeuner	to have lunch
un délice	delight
délicieuse	delicious
délicieux	delicious
demain	tomorrow
demander	to ask (for)
se demander	to wonder
bien démarrer	to get off to a good start
un déménagement	moving house
déménager	to move house
demi	half
un demi-frère	half-brother; step brother
une demi-journée	half-day
un demi-kilo	half a kilo
un demi-pensionnaire	pupil who stays at school for lunch
une demi-soeur	step sister; half sister

■ = masculine noun ■ = feminine noun ■ = verb ■ = adjective

et demie	half past (telling the time)
midi et demi	half past midday
une dent	tooth
un dentifrice	toothpaste
un dentiste	dentist
un départ	departure; starting point
un département	region (a bit like a county in Britain)
dépêche-toi (*from* se dépêcher)	hurry up
se dépêcher	to hurry up
dépêchez-vous (*from* se dépêcher)	hurry up
cela dépend (*from* dépendre)	it depends
dépendre	to depend
dépenser	to spend (money)
des dépenses	costs; expenditure
dépensier	extravagant
dépensière	extravagant
se déplacer	to get around; to move
un déplantoir	trowel
un dépliant	leaflet
déprimé	depressed
déprogrammé	cancelled
depuis	since; for
depuis un an	for a year
un dériveur	dinghy
dernier	last; latest
dernière	last; latest
des	some
dès	from
désagréable	nasty; unpleasant
descendre	to get off; to come down; to go down
une descente	landing
une description	description
un désert	desert
désespéré	desperate
au désespoir	in despair
désirer	to want; to wish for
désolé	sorry
un désordre	disorder; mess
désormais	from now on
un dessert	pudding
un dessin	drawing; art
un dessin animé	cartoon
un dessinateur	designer; artist; illustrator

dessiner	to draw
dessous	underneath
dessus	above
à destination de	going to
un détail	detail
des détails supplémentaires	extra information
détester	to hate; to detest
en détresse	in distress
un détroit	strait
deux	two
un deux-roues	two-wheeler
deuxième	second
je/tu devais (*from* devoir)	I/you should
devant	in front of
devenir	to become
deviner	to guess
une devinette	puzzle; riddle
une devise	motto; slogan; currency
devoir	to have to; must
des devoirs	homework
tu devrais (*from* devoir)	you ought to
un diabolo-menthe	fizzy mint drink
un diagramme	diagram
diamétralement	diametrically
un diamètre	diameter
une diapositive	colour slide
un dico	dictionary
un dictionnaire	dictionary
Dieu	God
un dieu	god
mon dieu!	goodness me!
des dieux	gods
une différence	difference
différent	different
difficile	difficult
une difficulté	problem
difforme	deformed
dimanche	Sunday
un dîner	dinner; evening meal
dîner	to dine; to eat a main meal
dingue	crazy
dire	to tell; to say
c'est-à- dire	in other words
veut dire (*from* vouloir)	means
direct	direct
en direct	live

■ = masculine noun ■ = feminine noun ■ = verb ■ = adjective

directement	straight
un directeur	director; headteacher
une direction	direction
une directrice	director; head teacher (female)
je dis (*from* dire)	I say
dis donc (*from* dire)	tell me
une discothèque	disco
discuter	to chat; to discuss
ils/elles disent (*from* dire)	they say
disparaître	to disappear
disparu	disappeared
disposer de	to have; to use
une dispute	quarrel
se disputer	to argue
un disque	record
une disquette	computer disk
dissimulé	hidden
distingué	distinguished
une distraction	entertainment
distrait	absent-minded
distribuer	to hand out; to deliver
il/elle dit (*from* dire)	he/she says
divers	various
diviser	to divide
divorcé	divorced
dix	ten
dix-huit	eighteen
dix-neuf	nineteen
dix-sept	seventeen
une djellaba	jellaba (item of clothing)
un docteur	doctor
une doctoresse	doctor
un documentaire	documentary
un dodo	sleep
un doigt	finger
des doigts de pied	toes
je dois (*from* devoir)	I must
il/elle doit (*from* devoir)	he/she should; must
un domestique	servant
dominer	to overlook; to dominate
un domino	domino
un dommage	pity
dommage!; quel dommage!	what a pity!
donc	so; therefore
donner	to give

dont	whose; of which
dormir	to sleep
je dors (*from* dormir)	I sleep
il/elle dort (*from* dormir)	he/she sleeps
un dortoir	dormitory
un dos	back
un dossier	project; file; folder
double	double
doublé	dubbed
eau douce	fresh water
douce	gentle; sweet; soft
doucement	slowly; gently
une douche	shower
se doucher	to have a shower
doué	gifted; good
pas de doute	no doubt
Douvres	Dover
doux	gentle; sweet; soft
une douzaine	dozen
douze	twelve
une dragée	sugared almond
une draisienne	hobby-horse
un drapeau	flag
une drogue	drug
drogué	drugged
une droguerie	hardware store
droit	straight
tout droit	straight on
à droite	on the right
la droite	right
droitier	right-handed
droitière	right-handed
drôle	funny
du	some; of the
un duc	duke
dur	hard
durer	to last
dynamique	dynamic
une dynamo	dynamo

E

l' eau	water
un éboueur	dustman
une échalote	shallot
un échange	exchange
faire un échange	to go on an exchange
échanger	to exchange; to swap
une écharpe	scarf
des échasses	stilts
s' échauffer	to warm up
les échecs	chess
jouer aux échecs	to play chess
une échelle	ladder
un échiquier	chess board
un éclair	kind of cake; lightning
un éclairage	lighting
une éclaircie	sunny period
éclairer	to light up
une école	school
une école du soir	night school
une école maternelle	nursery school
une école primaire	primary school
un écolier	schoolboy
une écolière	schoolgirl
l' écologie	ecology
économe	thrifty
faire des économies	to save up; to economise
économique	cheap
une écorce	bark
écossais	Scots; Scottish
l' Écosse	Scotland
écouter	to listen to
un écran	screen
écrasé	squashed
écrire	to write
s' écrire	to be spelt; to be written
Cela s' écrit comment? (*from* écrire)	How do you spell that?
une écriture	writing; handwriting
écrivez (*from* écrire)	write
un écrou	nut
s' écrouler	to crumble
un écusson	badge; shield
un édito	editorial

■ = masculine noun ■ = feminine noun ■ = verb ■ = adjective

l' éducation civique	civics; general studies; P.S.E.
l' éducation physique	physical education
un effort	effort
effrayant	frightening
égal	equal
égaler	to be equal to
l' égalité	equality
une église	church
égoïste	selfish
eh bien	well
un électricien	electrician
électroménager	household electrical
électroménagère	household electrical
un électrophone	record player
élégant	elegant
un éléphant	elephant
un élève	pupil
une élève	pupil
élever	to raise; to lift up
éliminer	to eliminate; to knock out; to rule out
elle	she; it; her
elles	they (feminine)
éloigner	to take away; to remove
un emballage	packaging; wrapping
embarquer	to get on board
embêtant	annoying; upsetting
embêter	to annoy
d' emblée	straight away; at once
un embouteillage	traffic jam
s' embrasser	to kiss
une émission	(TV) programme
emmener	to take (somebody somewhere)
l' emmental	kind of cheese
un emplacement	place; pitch for a tent
un emploi	job
un emploi du temps	school timetable
un employé	member of staff
une employée	member of staff
employer	to employ; to use
empoisonné	poisoned
emporter	to take away
une empreinte	footprint
emprunter	to borrow
l' E.M.T.	craft, design and technology

■ = masculine noun ■ = feminine noun ■ = verb ■ = adjective

en	in; on; made in
en coton	cotton
en effet	in fact
en face de	opposite
en fait	in fact
en forme	on form
en retard	late
en route	on the way; let's go!
enchanté	pleased to meet you
une vente aux enchères	auction
encore	still; more; again
encore un(e)	another
encourager	to encourage
endormi	sleepy; asleep
s' endormir	to fall asleep
un endroit	place
au bon endroit	in the right place
une énergie	energy
énergique	energetic
énervant	annoying
ça m' énerve	it annoys me
énervé	stimulated; irritated; annoyed
énerver	to get on someone's nerves
une enfance	childhood
un enfant	child
une enfant	child
un enfant unique	only child
d' enfer	'cool'
un enfer	hell
enfermé	shut in; enclosed
enfin	at last; anyway
s' enfoncer	to sink in
un engin	device
un engin spatial	spaceship
enlever	to take off; to remove
il s' ennuie (*from* ennuyer)	he's bored
s' ennuyer	to be bored
ennuyer	to bore
ennuyeuse	boring
ennuyeux	boring
énorme	enormous; huge
énormément	enormously
énormément de	lots of
une enquête	survey; inquiry; investigation
un enregistrement	recording
enregistrer	to record

■ = masculine noun ■ = feminine noun ■ = verb ■ = adjective

enrhumé	full of cold
être enrhumé	to have a cold
un enseignement	education
ensemble	together
ensoleillé	sunny
ensuite	next; then
entendre	to hear
s' entendre avec	to get on with
s' entendre bien (avec...)	to get on well (with...)
une entente	understanding
un enterrement	funeral
enthousiasmé	keen
enthousiaste	enthusiastic
entier	whole
entière	whole
entouré de	surrounded by
entourer	to surround
un entracte	interval
un entraînement	training
s' entraîner	to train
un entraîneur	trainer; coach
entre	between
une entrée	starter; entrance; entrance hall
une entreprise	firm; company
entrer	to go in; to enter
entretemps	meanwhile
une enveloppe	envelope
enveloppé	wrapped
à l' envers	upside down; inside out
un envers	wrong side
avoir envie de	to want to
environ	about
des environs	surrounding area
envoyer	to send
une épaule	shoulder
épeler	to spell
une épicerie	food shop; grocer's
des épices	spices
des épinards	spinach
une épingle de sûreté	safety pin
une épinglette	pin; badge
une épluchure	peeling
une éponge	sponge
une époque	time; era; period
un film d' épouvante	horror film

■ = masculine noun ■ = feminine noun ■ = verb ■ = adjective

des époux	husband and wife; married couple
l' E.P.S.	physical education
l' équateur	Equator
un équilibre	balance
équilibré	balanced
une équipe	team
une équipe de nuit	night shift
l' équipement	equipment; facilities
des équipements agricoles	farm equipment
des équipements scolaires	school equipment; school facilities
l' équitation	horse-riding
faire de l' équitation	to go horse riding
un équivalent	equivalent
une erreur	mistake
par erreur	by mistake
tu es (*from* être)	you are
l' escalade	rock climbing
un escalier	(flight of) stairs
un escalier mécanique	escalator
un escalier roulant	escalator
un escargot	snail
un esclave	slave
l' escrime	fencing
un espace	space
un espace vert	green/unspoilt area
l' Espagne	Spain
espagnol	Spanish
une espèce	kind of...; species
espérer	to hope
l' espionnage	spying
un esquimau	choc-ice
essayer de	to try to
l' essence	petrol
essuyer	to wipe
l' est	east
est (*from* être)	is
un estomac	stomach
et	and
et avec ceci?	anything else?
et bien	well
et demie	half past (telling the time)
et quart	quarter past (telling the time)
un étage	floor; storey
une étagère	bookshelf; shelf

■ = masculine noun ■ = feminine noun ■ = verb ■ = adjective

j' étais (*from* être)	I was
était (*from* être)	was
étaler	to spread
une étape	stage
un état	state
les États-Unis	United States
un été	summer
en été	in Summer
été (*from* être)	been
éteignez (*from* éteindre)	put out
éteindre	to put out; to switch off
éternuer	to sneeze
vous êtes (*from* être)	you are
une étiquette	label
une étoile	star
s' étonner	to be surprised
étourdi	scatter-brained
étrange	strange
un étranger	foreigner; stranger
étranger	foreign
à l' étranger	abroad
une étrangère	foreigner; stranger
étrangère	foreign
être	to be
étroit	narrow
une étude	private study
un étudiant	student
une étudiante	student
étudier	to study
eu (*from* avoir)	had
euh	er...
un eurochèque	eurocheque
eux	them
évaluer	to evaluate; to assess
une évasion	escape
un événement sportif	sporting event
un éventail	fan
un évier	kitchen sink
éviter	to avoid
exactement	exactly
exagérer	to exaggerate
une excursion	excursion; trip
excuser	to excuse
excusez-moi	excuse me; sorry
un exemple	example
par exemple	for example

■ = masculine noun ■ = feminine noun ■ = verb ■ = adjective

un **exercice**	exercise
un **expéditeur**	sender
une **expérience**	experience; experiment
expirer	to breathe out
expliquer	to explain
un **explorateur**	explorer
exploser	to explode
une **explosion**	explosion
une **exposition**	an exhibition
exprès	on purpose
une **expression**	expression
exprimer	to express
un **extérieur**	outside
à l' **extérieur**	outside; away from home
extra (***never changes***)	special; fantastic
un **extrait**	an extract
extraordinaire	extraordinary; amazing
extraverti	extrovert

F

une fabrication	production
une fabrique	factory
fabriqué	made
fabriquer	to make
qu'est-ce que tu fabriques?	what on earth are you up to?
une face	heads (on coin)
face à	facing; opposite
en face de	opposite
se fâcher	to get angry
facile	easy
facilement	easily
une façon	way; method
de toute façon	anyway
façonner	to shape; to mould
un facteur	postman
faible	feeble; weak
avoir faim	to be hungry
fainéant	lazy
faire	to do; to make
faire attention	to be careful
faire bonjour	to wave
faire confiance	to trust
faire connaissance	to meet
faire de la planche à voile	to go windsurfing
faire de la voile	to go sailing
faire des achats	to go shopping
faire des bêtises	to do silly things
faire des claquettes	to tap dance
faire des courses	to do the shopping
faire du bricolage	to do odd jobs
faire du chahut	to create an uproar
faire du jardinage	to do some gardening
faire du vélo	to go for a bike ride
faire l'imbécile	to be silly
faire la cuisine	to cook
faire la fête	to have a party
faire la lessive	to do the washing
faire la queue	to queue up
faire la vaisselle	to do the washing up
faire le lit	to make the bed
faire les courses	to do the shopping
faire les magasins	to go shopping

■ = masculine noun ■ = feminine noun ■ = verb ■ = adjective

faire partie de	to belong to
faire sa valise	to pack a suitcase
faire un régime	to go on a diet
faire un tour	to go for a walk/ride
faire une promenade	to go for a walk
un faire-part	announcement card
fais (*from* faire)	make; do
ne t'en fais pas	don't worry about it
en fait	in fact
il/elle fait (*from* faire)	he/she makes; does
il fait beau	it's nice (weather)
il fait chaud	it's hot
il fait du brouillard	it's foggy
il fait du soleil	its sunny
il fait du vent	it's windy
il fait froid	it's cold
il fait gris	it's overcast
il fait mauvais	it's bad weather
ça ne fait rien	it doesn't matter
faites (*from* faire)	make; do
familier	familiar
familière	familiar
une famille	family
en famille	with the family; as a family
un fan-club	fan club
un fana	fan
fantastique	fantastic
un fantôme	ghost
farci	stuffed
le fard	make-up
farfelu	scatty; eccentric
la farine	flour
fatigant	tiring
la fatigue	tiredness
fatigué	tired
la faune	wildlife
fausse	false; wrong
il faut (*from* falloir)	you have to; it is necessary to
il vous faut (*from* falloir)	you need
une faute	fault; mistake
un fauteuil	armchair
faux	false; wrong
favori	favourite
favorite	favourite
un féculent	starchy food
des félicitations	congratulations

■ = masculine noun ■ = feminine noun ■ = verb ■ = adjective

une femme	woman; wife
une femme d'affaires	businesswoman
une femme de ménage	cleaning lady
une fenêtre	window
un fer (à repasser)	an iron
un jour férié	public holiday; bank holiday
une ferme	farm
fermé	closed
fermer	to close; to shut
la fermeture annuelle	annual closing; yearly holidays
un fermier	farmer
féroce	fierce
une fesse	buttock
une fête	special day; celebration; festival
faire la fête	to celebrate
une fête foraine	fair
bonne fête!	happy name day!
fêter	to celebrate
un feu	light; fire
un feu d'artifice	firework display
une feuille	leaf; sheet of paper
un feuilleton	serial; soap opera
un feutre	felt-tip pen
des feux	traffic lights
février	February
un fiancé	fiancé
une fiancée	fiancée
une ficelle	thin French loaf
une fiche	worksheet; form
fidèle	faithful
fier	proud
fière	proud
une fièvre	temperature
fiévreuse	feverish
fiévreux	feverish
une figure	diagram; face
figurer	to feature
figurez-vous!	imagine!
un fil	wire
filer	to fly by
un filet	net
une fille	girl; daughter
une fille unique	only daughter; only child
un film	film

■ = masculine noun ■ = feminine noun ■ = verb ■ = adjective

un film d'horreur	horror film
un fils	son
un fils unique	only son; only child
une fin	end; finish
en fin de compte	when all is said and done
finalement	finally
fini	finished
finir	to finish; to end
fixe	unmoving; fixed; set
un flageolet	kidney bean
un flash-grammaire	grammar section
une flèche	arrow
une fleur	flower
un fleuriste	florist
un fleuve	(large) river
un flic	policeman (slang)
un flipper	pinball machine
flotter	to float
un flotteur	float
fluo	fluorescent
fluorescent	fluorescent
une flûte à bec	recorder
une fois	time; once
des fois	sometimes
à la fois	at the same time; at once
combien de fois?	how often?
folklorique	folk
folle	mad; crazy
foncé	dark
un fonctionnaire	civil servant
fonctionner	to work
un fond	bottom; back
au fond	basically
un fond de teint	foundation (make-up)
fonder	to found
(faire) fondre	to melt
ils font (*from* faire)	they do; they're doing
le foot	football
le football	football
un footing	jogging; jog
une forêt	forest
une forme	form; shape
avoir la forme	to be in good form
être en pleine forme	to be right on form
en forme	fit; in shape
former	to make up

formidable	great; tremendous
un formulaire	form
un formulaire de patronnage	sponsorship form
fort	strong; good at
il est fort en maths	he's good at maths
fortement	deeply; strongly
fou	mad; crazy
fouiller	to search; to rummage through; to dig
un foulard	scarf
un four (à micro-ondes)	(microwave) oven
au four	in the oven
une fourche	garden fork
une fourchette	fork
une fourmi	ant
fragile	fragile; delicate
fraîche	fresh; cool
frais	fresh; cool
une fraise	strawberry
une framboise	raspberry
un franc	franc
un Français	Frenchman
le français	French (the language)
français	French
une Française	Frenchwoman
la France	France
franchement	frankly
francophone	French-speaking
frapper	to knock; to hit
une fraternité	brotherhood
un frein	brake
freiner	to brake
un frère	brother
un frigo	fridge
un frimeur	show-off
des fringues	clothes (slang)
frisé	curly
un frisson	shiver; thrill
froid	cold
avoir froid	to feel cold
faire froid	to be cold
un fromage	cheese
un fromage blanc	soft white cheese
un front	forehead
une frontière	border
un fruit	fruit

■ = masculine noun ■ = feminine noun ■ = verb ■ = adjective

des fruits de mer	seafood
des fruits secs	dried fruit
la fumée	smoke
fumer	to smoke
un fumeur	smoker
une fumeuse	smoker
un funiculaire	funicular railway
furieuse	furious; angry
furieux	furious; angry
un fuseau horaire	time zone
une fusée	rocket

G

le Gabon	Gabon
un gagnant	winner
gagner	to win; to earn; to gain
une galerie d'art	art gallery
une galerie des glaces	hall of mirrors
une galette	savoury pancake
le pays de Galles	Wales
gallois	Welsh
galoper	to gallop
un gant	glove
un gant de boxe	boxing glove
un gant de toilette	flannel; wash glove
un garage	garage
un garçon	boy; waiter
garder	to keep; to look after
un gardien	warder; guard
une gare	station
une gare routière	bus station
garer	to park
un gars	lad; bloke
gâté	spoilt
un gâteau	cake; biscuit
un gâteau sec	biscuit
à gauche	on the left
gaucher	left-handed
gauchère	left-handed
une gaufre	waffle
un Gaulois	Gaul
un gaz	gas
gazeuse	fizzy
gazeux	fizzy
un gazon	lawn
un géant	giant
il gèle (*from* geler)	it's freezing
geler	to freeze
Gémeaux	Gemini
gênant	embarrassing
un gendarme	policeman
une gendarmerie	police-station
en général	usually
généralement	normally
un généraliste	GP
généreuse	generous

■ = masculine noun ■ = feminine noun ■ = verb ■ = adjective

généreux	generous
la génétique	genetics
génial	brilliant
un génie	genius
un genou	knee
une genouillère	knee-pad
des genoux	knees
un genre	type; kind
des gens	people
gentil	kind; nice
gentille	kind; nice
une gentillesse	kindness
la géographie	geography
une gerboise	gerbil
un geste	movement; gesture
gigantesque	gigantic
un gilet de sauvetage	lifejacket
une girafe	giraffe
une glace	ice cream; ice; mirror
un glaçon	ice cube
glisser	to slip; to slide
un globe	globe
la gloire	glory
une gomina	hair gel; hair cream
une gomme	rubber
une gorge	throat
un gorille	gorilla
un gosse	brat; kid
goudronné	tarred; made-up (a road)
une gourde	water bottle; flask
gourmand	greedy
un goût	taste
un goûter	afternoon snack
goûter	to taste
un gouvernement	government
grâce à	thanks to
un gradin	tier (of seating)
graisser	to grease
une grammaire	grammar
un gramme	gramme
grand	big; tall; large
grand-chose	much
une grand-mère	grand mother
un grand-père	grandfather
une grand-rue	high street
la Grande-Bretagne	Great Britain

■ = masculine noun ■ = feminine noun ■ = verb ■ = adjective

des grands-parents	grandparents
une grange	barn
un graphique	graph
une grappe	bunch (of grapes)
gras	fat; greasy
grasse	fat; greasy
au gratin	with cheese
un gratte-ciel	skyscraper
gratuit	free
grave	serious
ce n'est pas grave	it doesn't matter
grec	Greek
la Grèce	Greece
grecque	Greek
un grenier	attic
une grenouille	frog
une grève	strike
griffer	to claw
grignoter	to nibble
une grille	grid; barred gate
grimper	to climb
la grippe	flu
gris	grey
grognon	grumpy
grognonne	grumpy
gros	big; fat
une groseille	redcurrant
grosse	big; fat
une grotte	cave
un groupe	group
un groupe scolaire	school party
le gruyère	kind of cheese
guadeloupéen	from Guadeloupe
une guêpe	wasp
une guerre	war
un guichet	ticket office; counter
un guide	guidebook; guide
un guidon	handlebars
une guitare	guitar
la gym rythmique et sportive	eurythmics
un gymnase	gymnasium
la gymnastique	gymnastics

H

s' habiller	to get dressed
un habitant	inhabitant
habiter	to live
une habitude	habit
d' habitude	usually
habituel	usual
habituelle	usual
le steak haché	minced meat; mince
un hachis parmentier	shepherd's pie
une haie	hedge
un hamburger	hamburger
un hamster	hamster
des hanches	hips
un handicap	handicap
un handicapé physique	physically handicapped person
une handicapée physique	physically handicapped person
un haricot	bean
un haricot vert	green bean
par hasard	by chance
en haut	upstairs
haut	high
à haute voix	aloud
une hauteur	height
hein?	eh? right? what?
hélas!	worse luck!; unfortunately
un hélicoptère	helicopter
l' herbe	grass
un hérisson	hedgehog
un héros	hero
hésiter	to hesitate
une heure	hour; o'clock
l' heure	time
de bonne heure	early
une heure de pointe	rush hour
quelle heure est-il?	what's the time?
heureuse	happy
heureusement	fortunately; luckily
heureux	happy
un hibou	owl
hier	yesterday

■ = masculine noun ■ = feminine noun ■ = verb ■ = adjective

hier soir	last night
un hippodrome	race-course
un hippopotame	hippopotamus
une hirondelle	swallow
l' histoire	history
une histoire	story
historique	old; historic
l' hiver	winter
en hiver	in winter
le hockey	hockey
hollandais	Dutch
un homme	man
un homme d'affaires	businessman
la Hongrie	Hungary
hongrois	Hungarian
honnête	honest
la honte	shame
avoir honte	to be ashamed
un hôpital	hospital
des hôpitaux	hospitals
le hoquet	hiccoughs
un horaire	timetable
horizontalement	across (in a crossword)
une horloge	clock
un horloger	jeweller's; watchmaker
un horoscope	horoscope
avoir horreur de	to hate
j'ai horreur de ça	I can't stand that
horrible	awful; horrible
un hot-dog	hot dog
un hôtel	hotel
un hôtel de ville	town hall
un hôtelier	hotel-keeper
H.S. (hors service)	out of order
l' huile	oil
huit	eight
humain	human
humanitaire	humanitarian
de bonne humeur	in a good mood
une humeur	mood
humide	damp
hyper	very
un hypermarché	hypermarket

I

ici	here
par ici	this way
l' Id-al Fitr	Eid-ul Fitr
idéal	ideal
une idée	idea
identifier	to identify
une identité	identity
idiot	stupid; idiotic
il y a	there is/are
une île	island
les îles anglo-normandes	Channel Islands
illuminé	lit up; illuminated
illustrer	to illustrate
ils	they
une image	picture
imaginaire	imaginary
imaginer	to imagine
imbattable	unbeatable
un imbécile	idiot
une imbécile	idiot
faire l' imbécile	to be silly
imbécile	stupid
imiter	to imitate
immédiatement	immediately
un immeuble	block of flats
un impasse	dead end; cul de sac
un imperméable	raincoat
impoli	impolite; rude
important	important
n' importe quel	any
n' importe quoi	anything; no matter what
impossible	impossible
impressionnant	impressive
impressionner	to impress
des imprimés	printed matter
un incendie	fire
un incident	incident
inconnu	unknown
un inconvénient	disadvantage
incroyable	unbelievable
incroyablement	incredibly
l' Inde	India
indépendant	independent

un index	forefinger; index finger
un indicatif	dialling code
un indice	clue
indiquer	to indicate; to show
infect	horrible
inférieur	lower
une infirmerie	sick bay; medical centre
un infirmier	nurse
une infirmière	nurse
influencer	to influence
un informaticien	computer programmer
une informaticienne	computer programmer
les informations	news
l' informatique	computer studies; IT
un ingénieur	engineer
un ingrédient	ingredient
inquiet	worried; anxious
inquiète	worried; anxious
ne t' inquiète pas	don't worry
un insecte	insect
insolent	cheeky
insomniaque	insomniac; unable to sleep
un inspecteur	inspector
inspirer	to breathe in
s' installer	to settle down; to sit
un instant	moment
pour l' instant	at the moment
instinctivement	instinctively
une instruction	instruction; education
l' instruction civique	social studies; PSE
l' instruction religieuse	religious education
un instrument de musique	musical instrument
insupportable	unbearable
intellectuel	intellectual
intellectuelle	intellectual
intelligent	clever
interdit	forbidden; not allowed
il est interdit de	you are not allowed to
intéressant	interesting
intéresser	to interest
s' intéresser à	to be interested in
un intérêt	interest
un intérieur	inside
un internat	boarding school
un interne	boarder
une interne	boarder

■ = masculine noun ■ = feminine noun ■ = verb ■ = adjective

un interprète	an interpreter
une interprète	an interpreter
une interro(gation)	test
une interview	interview
interviewer	to interview
intitulé	entitled; called
un intrus	odd one out
inventer	to invent
une invitation	invitation
inviter	to invite
irlandais	Irish
l' Irlande	Ireland
irritant	irritating
irrité	irritated
irriter	to irritate
isolé	isolated; lonely
l' Italie	Italy
italien	Italian
italienne	Italian
en italique	in italics
un itinéraire	route; itinerary
la Côte d' Ivoire	Ivory Coast
l' ivoire	ivory
un Ivoirien	an inhabitant of the Ivory Coast
une Ivoirienne	an inhabitant of the Ivory Coast

■ = masculine noun ■ = feminine noun ■ = verb ■ = adjective

J

jalouse	jealous
jaloux	jealous
jamaïcain	Jamaican
la Jamaïque	Jamaica
jamais	never
une jambe	leg
un jambon	ham
janvier	January
le Japon	Japan
japonais	Japanese
un jardin	garden
un jardin des plantes	botanical gardens
un jardin public	park
le jardinage	gardening
jaune	yellow
un javelot	javelin
je	I
un jean	pair of jeans
les Jersiais	Jersey people
jeter	throw
un jeton	counter
un jeu	game; quiz
un jeu de l'oie	snakes and ladders
un jeu de société	board game
un jeu vidéo	video game
un jeu-test	quiz
jeudi	Thursday
jeune	young
les jeunes	young people
les Jeux Olympiques	Olympic Games
la Joconde	Mona Lisa
un jogging	tracksuit; jogging
une joie	joy
joignez une photo (*from* joindre)	enclose a photo
joindre	to join; to attach
joli	pretty
une jonquille	daffodil
une joue	cheek
jouer	play
un jouet	toy
un joueur	player
un jour	day

■ = masculine noun ■ = feminine noun ■ = verb ■ = adjective

par jour	per day
un jour de congé	day off
le jour de Noël	Christmas Day
le jour-J	D-Day
un journal	diary; newspaper
un journaliste	journalist
une journaliste	journalist
une journée	day
tous les jours	every day
joyeuse	happy
joyeux	happy
le judo	judo
juger	judge
juif	Jewish
juillet	July
juin	June
juive	Jewish
un jumeau	male twin
un jumelage	(town) twinning
jumelé	twinned
une jumelle	female twin
des jumelles	twins; binoculars
une jupe	skirt
un jury	jury
un jus	juice
un jus d'orange	orange juice
un jus de fruit	fruit juice
jusqu'à	until; as far as
un justaucorps	body stocking
juste	right; correct; fair
juste à temps	just in time

K

un **kangourou**	kangaroo
le **karaté**	karate
un **kilo**	kilo
un **kilomètre**	kilometre
kilomètre à l'heure	km/h
un **kimono**	kimono
un **kiosque**	kiosk

L

la	the
là	there
là-bas	over there
là-dedans	in there
un labo(ratoire)	lab(oratory)
un lac	lake
laid	ugly
la laine	wool
en laine	made of wool
une laisse	lead
laisser	to leave; to let
laisser tomber	to drop
le lait	milk
le lait de soleil	sun-tan lotion
le lait en poudre	powdered milk
le lait solaire	sun cream
laitier	made from milk
laitière	made from milk
une laitue	lettuce
une lampe	lamp
une lampe de poche	torch
lancer	to throw
un langage	language
une langoustine	prawn
une langue	language; tongue
une langue étrangère	foreign language
un lapin	rabbit
laquelle	which
large	wide
un laurier	laurel
un lavabo	washbasin
la lavande	lavender
un lave-vaisselle	dish-washer
se laver	to get washed
laver	to wash
lécher	to lick
une leçon	lesson
un lecteur	reader
une lectrice	reader
la lecture	reading
bonne lecture!	good reading!
légendaire	legendary
une légende	caption; key (to a map)

■ = masculine noun ■ = feminine noun ■ = verb ■ = adjective

léger	light
légère	light
un légume	vegetable
le lendemain	next day
lent	slow
lentement	slowly
lequel	which
les	the
lesquelles	which
la lessive	washing
une lettre	letter
leur	their
une levée	collection (of letters)
se lever	to get up
lever	to raise; to lift
levez-vous (*from* se lever)	stand up
une lèvre	lip
une levure	raising agent; yeast
un lexique	vocabulary list
une liberté	freedom
une librairie	bookshop
libre	free; vacant
un lien	bond; lien
un lieu	place
au lieu de	instead of
un lièvre	hare
une ligne	line
une ligne aérienne	airline
une ligue	league
lilas	lilac
une limonade	lemonade
un lion	lion
un liquide	liquid
lire	to read
je lis (*from* lire)	I read
lisez! (*from* lire)	read!
lisse	smooth
une liste	list
un lit	bed
un lit de camp	camp bed
il/elle lit (*from* lire)	he/she reads
un lit superposé	bunk bed
un litre	litre
un livre	book
une livre	pound (weight and sterling)
un livre d'élève	pupil's book

■ = masculine noun ■ = feminine noun ■ = verb ■ = adjective

livrer	to deliver
un livret de caisse d'épargne	savings account
local	local
un location	hire
logé	housed
un loge de concierge	caretaker's office
le logement	housing
logique	logical
c'est loin	it is far away
lointain	distant
un loisir	leisure activity
Londres	London
long	long
longtemps	long time
longue	long
une longueur	length
un look	look; style
une loterie	lottery
un lotissement	housing estate
le Loto	Bingo
une louche	ladle
louer	to rent; to hire
loufoque	crazy; barmy
un loup	wolf
une loupe	magnifying glass
lourd	heavy
lu (*from* lire)	read
une luge	toboggan
lui	him; her; to him; to her
une lumière	light
lundi	Monday
une lune	moon
une lunette	telescope
des lunettes	glasses; spectacles
des lunettes de soleil	sunglasses
un lutin	imp
la lutte	wrestling
lutter	to fight
un luxe	luxury
de luxe	luxury
le Luxembourg	Luxembourg
un lycée	upper secondary school; sixth form college
un lycéen	sixth former (roughly)
une lycéenne	sixth former (roughly)

■ = masculine noun ■ = feminine noun ■ = verb ■ = adjective

M

M.	= monsieur (Mr.)
ma	my (feminine)
un macaron	badge
une macédoine de fruits	fruit salad
un machin	thingy; whatsit
une machine	machine
une machine à laver	washing machine
une machine à traitement de textes	word processor
un maçon	builder
Madame	Mrs
Mademoiselle	Miss
un magasin	shop
un grand magasin	department store
un magazine	magazine
la magie	magic
magique	magic
un magnétophone	tape recorder
un magnétoscope	video recorder
magnifique	magnificent
mai	May
maigre	thin
maigrir	to lose weight; to slim
un maillot	(sports) jersey; shirt
un maillot de bain	swimming costume; trunks
une main	hand
à la main	by hand
maintenant	now
un maire	mayor
une mairie	town hall
mais	but
le maïs	maize
le maïs doux	sweetcorn
une maison	house
à la maison	at home
une maison des jeunes	youth centre
un maître	(school) master
une maîtresse	(school) mistress
mal	bad; badly
pas mal	not bad
avoir mal	to hurt; to feel ill
ça fait mal	it hurts
j'ai mal à la tête	I've got a headache

■ = masculine noun ■ = feminine noun ■ = verb ■ = adjective

j'ai mal au coeur	I feel sick
le mal de mer	seasickness
mal élevé	bad mannered
malade	sick; ill
un malade	patient
une malade	patient
une maladie	illness; sickness
maladroit	clumsy
malgache	Malagasy
un malheur	misfortune; unhappiness
malheureuse	unhappy
malheureusement	unfortunately
malheureux	unhappy
maligne	crafty; mischievous
malin	crafty; mischievous
maman	mum
mamie	gran
la Manche	English Channel
une manche	handle
un mandat	order
un manège	roundabout
manger	to eat
une salle manger	dining room
une mangue	mango
des manières	manners
une manif(estation)	demonstration
manoeuvrer	to steer
il manque ...	there isn't/aren't enough ...
manquer	to miss; to be missing
manquer à	to be missed by
une mansarde	attic room
un manteau	coat; overcoat
un maquereau	mackerel
une maquette	model; model-making
le maquillage	make-up
se maquiller	to put on make-up
un marchand	shopkeeper; stallholder
des marchandises	goods
une marche	step; stair; walking
un marché	market
un marché aux puces	flea market
marcher	to walk
mardi	Tuesday
Mardi gras	Shrove Tuesday
un mari	husband
un mariage	wedding; marriage

marié	married
marier	to marry
un marin	sailor
une marionnette	puppet
le Maroc	Morocco
marocain	Moroccan
une marotte	life-size puppet; dummy
une marque	brandname; make
marquer	to score
marrant	funny
j'en ai marre	I'm fed up
marron	chestnut brown
mars	March
la Marseillaise	French national anthem
un marteau	hammer
un masque	mask
un mât	mast
un match de foot	football match
un matelas pneumatique	airbed
un matériel	equipment
les mathématiques	mathematics
les maths	maths
une matière	school subject
la matière grasse	fat
un matin	morning
matinal	in the morning
une matinée	morning
l'île Maurice	Mauritius
mauvais	bad; wrong
il fait mauvais	the weather is poor
mauve	mauve
une mayonnaise	salad cream
me	me; myself
un mec	guy; bloke (slang)
un mécanicien	mechanic
une mécanicienne	mechanic
la mécanique	mechanics; workings
méchant	naughty; vicious
un méchoui	North African barbecue meal
mécontent	discontented; annoyed
une médaille	medal
un médecin	doctor
médical	medical
un médicament	medicine
médiéval	medieval
la Méditerranée	Mediterranean sea

■ = masculine noun ■ = feminine noun ■ = verb ■ = adjective

méfiant	distrustful; suspicious
se méfier de	to be wary of; to be suspicious of
meilleur	best
mélangé	mixed up; muddled up
mélanger	to mix
une mélasse	mess
un membre	member
une membre	member
mémé	grandma
même	same; even
une mémoire	memory
mémoriser	to memorise
menacer	to threaten
le ménage	household; housework
faire le ménage	to do the housework
une ménagère	housewife
mener	to lead
un menteur	liar
une menteuse	liar
la menthe	mint
mentionner	to mention
un menton	chin
une mer	sea
merci	thank you
mercredi	Wednesday
le mercurochrome	red antiseptic
une mère	mother
une belle-mère	stepmother
une merveille	marvel
merveilleuse	marvellous
merveilleux	marvellous
mes	my
mesdames	ladies
une messe	mass (in church)
messieurs	gentlemen
messieurs-dames	ladies and gentlemen
une mesure	measurement
mesurer	to measure
il/elle met (*from* mettre)	he/she puts on (clothes)
une météo	weather forecast
une méthode	method
un métier	job; occupation
un mètre	metre
un métro	underground railway
je mets (*from* mettre)	I put; I put on

■ = masculine noun ■ = feminine noun ■ = verb ■ = adjective

mettre	to put; to put on
mettre la table	to set the table
un meuble	piece of furniture
des meubles	furniture
un meurtre	murder
mi-long	mid-length
miam!	yum yum!
miaou	miaow
un micro	microphone
un microbe	microbe; germ
le Midi	South of France
midi	midday; noon
un miel	honey
le mien	mine
la mienne	mine
les miens	mine
les miennes	mine
mieux	better
mignon	cute; sweet
mignonne	cute; sweet
mijoter	to simmer
un milieu	middle
au milieu de	in the middle of
mille	thousand
un mille	mile
un milliard	thousand million; billion
des milliers de	thousands of
minable	pathetic; rubbish
mince	slim
mince!	oh no!; damn!
minéral	mineral
une mini-jupe	mini-skirt
le minitel	computerised telephone directory
minuit	midnight
minuscule	very small; tiny
une minute	minute
un miroir	mirror
mis (*from* mettre)	put; placed
misérable	wretched
un mite	clothes-moth grub
mité	moth-eaten
mixte	mixed
Mlle.	= Mademoiselle (Miss)
Mme.	= Madame (Mrs.)
une mobylette	moped

■ = masculine noun ■ = feminine noun ■ = verb ■ = adjective

moche	awful; ghastly
une mode	fashion
à la mode	in fashion
un modèle	model; example
le modélisme	model-making
modéré	moderate; calm; restrained
moderne	modern
moi	me
moi non plus	nor me; me neither
moins	less; minus
le moins	the least
au moins	at least
moins ... que	less ... than
moins de	less than
moins le quart	quarter to (time)
un mois	month
molle	soft
les Moluques	the Moluccas; the Spice Islands
un moment	moment
mon	my
un monde	world
beaucoup de monde	lots of people
tout le monde	everybody
il y a du monde	it's busy; it's crowded
un moniteur	instructor
une monitrice	instructor
la monnaie	change; coins; currency
Monsieur	Mr.; Sir
un monstre	monster
une montagne	mountain
montagneuse	mountainous
montagneux	mountainous
un montant	total amount
monter	to go up; to get in; to climb
monter à cheval	to go horse riding
une montgolfière	hot air balloon
une montre	watch
montrer	to show
un monument	sight
un moral	spirits
un morceau (de)	a piece (of)
mordre	to bite
le morpion	noughts and crosses
mort	dead
une mort	death

■ = masculine noun ■ = feminine noun ■ = verb ■ = adjective

une morve	mucus
une mosquée	mosque
un mot	word
un mot clé	key word
un motard	motorcyclist
un moteur	engine
une moto	motorbike
les mots croisés	crossword
mou	soft
une mouche	fly
un mouchoir	handkerchief
une moule	mussel
un moule	cake tin
une mousse au chocolat	chocolate mousse
une moustache	moustache
un moustique	mosquito
une moutarde	mustard
un mouton	sheep
un moyen	means
moyen	average; medium
le Moyen-Orient	Middle East
moyenne	average; medium
en moyenne	on average
moyennement	fairly; moderately
muet	silent; dumb
muette	silent; dumb
le muguet	lily of the valley
multiplié par	multiplied by
municipale	belonging to the town
une municipalité	municipality
un mur	wall
une muraille	wall
une mûre	blackberry
le muscadet	dry white wine
un muscle	muscle
musclé	muscular
la musculation	body-building
un musée	museum
un musicien	musician
une musicienne	musician
une musique	music
une mutinerie	mutiny
un mystère	mystery

■ = masculine noun ■ = feminine noun ■ = verb ■ = adjective

N

n'est-ce pas?	isn't that so?; right?
nager	to swim
un nain	dwarf
une naissance	birth
naître	to be born
nantais	from Nantes
une nappe	tablecloth
un napperon	tablemat
la natation	swimming
national	national
la nature	nature
naturel	natural
naturelle	natural
naturellement	of course
nautique	nautical; water
un navet	turnip; bad film
faire la navette	to operate a shuttle service
une navette	shuttle
un navigateur	navigator
né (*from* naître)	born
ne ... pas	not
ne ... que	only
ne ... ni ... ni	neither... nor... nor
ne ... plus	no more; no longer
ne ... rien	nothing
nécessaire	necessary
néerlandais	Dutch
la neige	snow
neiger	to snow
néo-zélandais	from New Zealand
un nerf	nerve
nerveuse	nervous
nerveux	nervous
nettoyer	to clean
neuf	nine
neuf	brand new
neuve	brand new
un neveu	nephew
un nez	nose
ni	neither; nor
une niche	kennel
une nièce	niece

■ = masculine noun ■ = feminine noun ■ = verb ■ = adjective

le Niger	the Niger
un niveau	level
nocturne	evening
Noé	Noah
Noël	Christmas
noir	black
une noix	nut
un nom	name
le nom (de famille)	surname
un nombre	number
nombreuse	numerous
nombreux	numerous
nommé	named
nommer	to name; to choose
non	no
non fumeur	non smoking
non fumeuse	non smoking
non lucratif	non profit-making
non lucrative	non profit-making
non plus	neither
le Nord	North
normal	normal; usual
normalement	normally
normand	Norman
la Normandie	Normandy
norvégien	Norwegian
norvégienne	Norwegian
nos	our
une note	bill; mark
noter	to jot down
notre	our
un nœud papillon	bow tie
des nouilles	noodles
un nounours	teddy bear
nourrir	to feed
une nourriture	food
nous	we; us
nouveau	new
une nouveauté	novelty
le nouvel an	the New Year
nouvelle	new
la Nouvelle-Calédonie	New Caledonia
la Nouvelle-Zélande	New Zealand
novembre	November
un nuage	cloud
une nuit	night

nul	useless; no good
il est nul en maths	he's useless at maths
nulle	useless; no good
un numéro	number; copy (of magazine)
un numéro d'immatriculation	registration number

O

un objet	object
un objet de valeur	valuable
des objets trouvés	lost property
obligatolre	compulsory
obliger de	to force to
un observateur	observer
observer	to watch
obstiné	obstinate; stubborn
obtenir	to obtain
à l' occasion de	at the time of
d' occasion	second-hand
occupé	busy; taken
s' occuper de	to look after
un océan	ocean
l' Océanie	Australasia
octobre	October
une odeur	smell
un oeil	eye
un oeuf	egg
offert (*from* offrir)	offered
un office de tourisme	tourist information office
une offre	offer
des offres d'emploi	situations vacant
offrir	to give (a gift)
ohé!	hey there!
une oie	goose
un oignon	onion
un oiseau	bird
une olive	olive
un olivier	olive tree
une ombre	shadow
une ombrelle	parasol; sunshade
une omelette	omelette
un omnibus	old word for bus
un oncle	uncle
ondulé	wavy
un ongle	fingernail
ils/elles ont (*from* avoir)	they have
onze	eleven
un opéra	opera (house)
une opération	operation
un ophtalmologiste	eye specialist
une opinion	opinion

opposé	opposite
l' or	gold
d' or	golden
un orage	storm
une orange	orange
un orangina	fizzy orange drink
un orchestre	orchestra
ordinaire	ordinary
un ordinateur	computer
un ordre	command
en ordre	tidy; in order
une oreille	ear
un organisateur	organiser
organiser	to organise
un organisme	organisation
originaire	native
original	original
l' ornithologie	bird watching
un orteil	toe
un os	bone
ou	or
où	where
ouah-ouah	woof-woof
ouais	yeah
oublier	to forget
l' ouest	west
un œuf	egg
ouf!	whew!
oui	yes
ourdou	Urdu
un ours	bear
outre-Rhin	beyond the Rhine
ouvert	open
une ouverture	opening
un ouvrage de référence	reference text
ouvre/ouvrez (*from* ouvrir)	open
un ouvre-boîtes	tin-opener
un ouvrier	worker; labourer
une ouvrière	worker; labourer
ouvrir	to open
l' oxygène	oxygen

■ = masculine noun ■ = feminine noun ■ = verb ■ = adjective

P

une page	page
pailleté	spangled; sequined
un pain	bread; loaf
le pain grillé	toast
une paire	pair
paisible	peaceful
un palais	palace
un palmier	palm tree
un panier	basket
un panier de provisions	shopping basket
paniquer	to panic
une panne	breakdown
en panne	broken down
une panne d'électricité	power failure; power cut
un panneau	sign
un panneau d'affichage	notice board
un pansement	dressing; plaster
un pantalon	trousers
une panthère	panther
le papa	dad
une papaye	pawpaw
le pape	Pope
une papeterie	stationer's
le papier	paper
en papier	made of paper
le papier à lettres	writing paper
le papier toilette	toilet paper
un papillon	butterfly
Pâques	Easter
un paquet	parcel; packet
par	by; through; with
par contre	however
par exemple	for example
par là	that way
par ordre	in order
par semaine	per week
le parachutisme	parachuting
paraître	to appear
un parapluie	umbrella
un parasol	beach umbrella; sunshade
un parc	park
un parc d'attractions	theme park
un parc-mètre	parking meter

■ = masculine noun ■ = feminine noun ■ = verb ■ = adjective

un parcours	route
pardon	excuse me
pardonner	to forgive
pareil	same; similar
pareille	same; similar
un parent	parent; relative
paresseuse	lazy
paresseux	lazy
parfait	perfect
parfois	sometimes
un parfum	flavour; perfume
parfumé	flavoured; scented
un parking	car park
parler	to talk; to speak
parmi	among
une paroisse	parish
une parole	word; speech
prendre la parole	to speak
À vous la parole!	Your turn to speak!
il/elle part (*from* partir)	he/she goes away
partager	to share
un partenaire	partner
une partenaire	partner
participer à	to take part in
particulier	particular; special
particulière	particular; special
une partie	part; some; game
faire partie de	to be a member of; to be a part of
partir	to leave; to go
à partir de	from
partir du bon pied	to get off to a good start
partout	everywhere
pas	not
pas d'accord	don't agree
pas du tout	not at all
pas grand-chose	not much
pas mal	not bad
un passage	passage; passing
un passage clouté	pedestrian crossing
un passage souterrain	subway
un passager	passenger
le passé	the past
un passe-temps	pastime; hobby
un passeport	passport

■ = masculine noun ■ = feminine noun ■ = verb ■ = adjective

passer	to spend (time); to show (a programme); to take (a test)
se passer	to happen
passer à	to go to; to move to
passer l'aspirateur	to hoover; to vacuum
passer un tour	to miss a turn
une passion	passion
passionnant	exciting
un passionné	fan
passionné	passionate
une passionnée	fan
passionnément	passionately
passionner	to interest
une pastille	lozenge
un pâte	pastry; cake mix
un pâté	pâté; meat paste
les pâtes	pasta
patiemment	patiently
une patience	patience
un patin	skate; brake block
le patin à glace	ice skating
le patin à roulettes	roller skating
le patinage	skating
le patinage artistique	ice dancing
patiner	to skate
une patinoire	ice-rink; skating rink
des patins à roulettes	roller skates
une pâtisserie	cake shop; cakes
un patron	boss; manager
le patronage	sponsorship
une patronne	boss; manager
une patte	paw; animal's foot
une paupière	eyelid
une pause	break
pauvre	poor
des pauvres	poor people
une pauvreté	poverty
payant	paying
payer	to pay
un pays	country
le Pays de Galles	Wales
les Pays-Bas	Holland; Netherlands
un paysage	landscape; countryside
une peau	skin
une pêche	peach; fishing
aller à la pêche	to go fishing

un péché mignon	weakness
un pêcheur	fisherman
un peigne	comb
un peignoir	dressing gown
peint	painted
un peintre	painter
une peintre	painter
une peinture	painting
peler	to peel
une pelle	spade
une pellicule	film (for a camera); dandruff
une pelouse	lawn
une peluche	soft toy
se pencher	to lean
pendant	during; for
pendant ce temps	meanwhile
le pendu	hangman (game)
une pendule	clock
pénible	tedious; irritating
une péniche	barge
penser (à)	to think (of)
une pension	boarding-house
la pension complète	full board
la Pentecôte	Whitsun
un pépé	grandad
le saut à la perche	pole vault
un perchoir	perch
un percolateur	coffee percolator
perdre	to lose
se perdre	to get lost
perdu	lost
un père	father
le père Noël	Father Christmas
une(salle de) permanence	study room; office
en permanence	in private study
permanent	permanent
un permis de conduire	driving licence
la permission	permission; leave
perpétuel	everlasting
perpétuelle	everlasting
un perroquet	parrot
une perruche	budgerigar
une perruque	wig
un personnage	famous person; character
une personne	person
ne ... personne	nobody

■ = masculine noun ■ = feminine noun ■ = verb ■ = adjective

un personnel	staff
peser	to weigh
la Pessah	Passover
pétillant	fizzy
petit	small; little
un petit ami	boyfriend
un petit déjeuner	breakfast
un petit pois	pea
un petit-fils	grandson
une petite amie	girlfriend
une petite-fille	granddaughter
des petits-enfants	grandchildren
un peu	a little; a few; a bit
peu à peu	little by little
à peu près	about; approximately
un peuple	people
une peur	fear
avoir peur de	to be afraid of
il/elle/on peut (*from* pouvoir)	he/she/we can
peut-être	perhaps; maybe
ils/elles peuvent (*from* pouvoir)	they can
je peux (*from* pouvoir)	I can
un phare	lighthouse; headlight
une pharmacie	chemist's
la philatélie	stamp collecting
un phoque	seal
le phosphore	phosphorus
phosphorescent	luminous
une photo	photograph
une photographe	photographer
un photographe	photographer
la photographie	photography
une phrase	sentence
des phrases-clés	key phrases
un physicien	physicist
la physique	physics
un piano	piano
picorer	to peck; to pick at food
un picoreur	someone who picks at food
une picoreuse	someone who picks at food
un pictogramme	picture puzzle
une pièce	room; coin; play
2 francs la pièce	2 francs each
une pièce d'identité	identification
un pied	foot
à pied	on foot

■ = masculine noun ■ = feminine noun ■ = verb ■ = adjective

une pierre	stone
un piéton	pedestrian
une pile	battery
pile	tails (on coin)
un pilote	pilot
une femme pilote	pilot
un pilote de rallye	rally driver
une femme pilote de rallye	rally driver
un pin	pine
un pin's	metal badge
pincer	to pinch
le ping-pong	table tennis
un pingouin	penguin
piocher	to pick up (a card)
un pique-nique	picnic
piquer	to sting; to pinch
une piqûre	bite; sting; injection
une piscine	swimming pool
une piscine couverte	indoor swimming pool
une pistache	pistachio nut
une piste	track; trail; skislope
une piste cyclable	cycle track
faire le pitre	to act the fool
pittoresque	picturesque
un placard	cupboard
une place	square; seat
sur place	on the spot
à la place de	instead of; in place of
une plage	beach
plaire à	to attract
plaisanter	to joke
un plaisir	pleasure
s'il te (vous) plaît	please
ça me plaît	I like it
un plan	map; plan
le gros plan	close-up view
une planche	board
une planche à repasser	ironing board
une planche à roulettes	skateboard
la planche à voile	windsurfing
un plancher	floor
une planète	planet
planifier	to plan
une plante	plant
une plaque	badge
une plaquette	door plate; nameplate

■ = masculine noun ■ = feminine noun ■ = verb ■ = adjective

plastique	plastic
un plat	dish; meal; course
à plat	flat
un plateau	tray
un plâtre	plaster
plein	full
en plein air	in the open air
en pleine forme	really fit
pleurer	to cry
il pleut (*from* pleuvoir)	it's raining
il pleuvait (*from* pleuvoir)	it was raining
pleuvoir	to rain
un pliant	folding campstool
plier	to fold; to bend
la plongée	diving
la plongée sous-marine	scuba diving
plonger	to dive
la pluie	rain
la pluie acide	acid rain
la plupart	most
le pluriel	plural
plus	more
en plus	besides that
non plus	neither
plus ... que	more ... than
plus de	more than (with numbers)
plus tard	later
plusieurs	several
plutôt	rather; instead
un pneu	tyre
une poche	pocket
une poêle	frying pan
un poème	poem
la poésie	poetry
un poète	poet
un poids	weight
un poil	hair
des poils	fur
un point	score; point; fullstop
un point d'eau	tap
un point de repère	landmark
une pointure	shoe size
une poire	pear
à pois	spotted
des petits pois	peas
un poisson	fish

■ = masculine noun ■ = feminine noun ■ = verb ■ = adjective

un poisson rouge	goldfish
une poissonnerie	fishmonger's
Poissons	Pisces
une poitrine	chest
le poivre	pepper
un poivron	pepper (vegetable)
poli	polite
un policier	police story; policeman
poliment	politely
polluant	polluting
pollué	polluted
une pollution	pollution
la Pologne	Poland
un polyglotte	speaker of many languages
une polyglotte	speaker of many languages
une pommade	cream
une pomme	apple
une pomme de pin	pine cone
une pomme de terre	potato
un pommier	apple tree
une pompe	pump
un pompier	fireman
un pont	bridge
populaire	popular
une population	population
le porc	pork
un porc-épics	porcupine
la porcelaine	china
une porcherie	pigsty
une porte	door; departure gate
un porte-clé	key ring
un porte-crayon	pencil case
un porte-manteau	coat rack
un porte-monnaie	purse
un portefeuille	wallet
porter	to wear; to carry
un portrait	portrait; profile
un portrait-robot	photofit picture
portugais	Portuguese
poser	to put down
poser une question	to ask a question
posséder	to have; to own
une possibilité	possibility
possible	possible
une poste	post office
un poste de police	police station

■ = masculine noun ■ = feminine noun ■ = verb ■ = adjective

un poste de TV	TV set
un poster	poster
un pot	pot
un potage	soup
un poteau	post; stake
une poubelle	dustbin
un pouce	thumb
une poule	hen
un poulet	chicken
un pouls	pulse
un poumon	lung
une poupée	doll
pour	for; in order to
pour cent	per cent
un pourboire	tip
pourquoi	why
je/tu pourrais (*from* pouvoir)	I/you could
il/elle/on pourrait (*from* pouvoir)	he/she/we could
un pousse-pousse	rick-shaw
pousser	to push
une poussière	dust
vous pouvez (*from* pouvoir)	you can
un pouvoir	power
pouvoir	to be able to
une prairie	meadow
pratique	useful; practical
pratiquer	to practise; to take part in
se précipiter	to hurry; to rush
précis	exactly
préféré	favourite
de préférénce	preferably
préférer	to prefer
premier	first
première	first
prendre	to take; to have; to eat
prendre feu	to catch fire
prendre un pot	to take a drink
je prends (*from* prendre)	I take
prenez (*from* prendre)	take
un prénom	first name; forename
nous prenons (*from* prendre)	we take
préparer	to prepare
se préparer à	to get ready to
près	near(by)
tout près	close; nearby
près de	near to

présenter	to introduce
se présenter à	to go to
un président	president
presque	nearly; almost
la presse	press
pressé	in a hurry
une pression	pressure
une bière pression	draught beer
prêt	ready
prêt-à-porter	ready-to-wear
prêter	to lend
une preuve	proof
prévenir	to warn
la prévention routière	road safety
des prévisions	forecast
prévoir	to plan; to anticipate
je vous en prie	don't mention it
prier	to request; to beg
principal	main
principalement	mainly
une principauté	principality
le printemps	spring
au printemps	in spring
pris (*from* prendre)	taken; had; eaten
une prise	plug; socket
un prisonnier	prisoner
privé	private
un prix	price; prize
un prix net	inclusive price
un problème	problem
prochain	next
producteur	producing
productrice	producing
produire	to produce
ils/elles produisent (*from* produire)	they produce
un produit	product
un prof	teacher
une prof	teacher
un professeur	teacher
une professeur	teacher
professionnel	professional
professionnelle	professional
un profil	profile
profiter de	to take advantage of
profond	deep
un programme informatique	computer program

■ = masculine noun ■ = feminine noun ■ = verb ■ = adjective

programmer	to program (computers)
le progrès	progress
un projet	plan
une promenade	walk; outing; ride
faire une promenade	to go for a walk
se promener	to go for a walk
promener le chien	to walk the dog
promis	promised
prononcer	to pronounce
à propos	by the way
proposer	to suggest
une proposition	suggestion
propre	clean; own
un propriétaire	owner
une propriétaire	owner
protéger	to protect
la protéine	protein
prouver	to prove
provoquer	to cause; to provoke
prudent	careful
un psychiatre	psychiatrist
PTT	post office
pu (*from* pouvoir)	could
une pub(licité)	advertising; advertisement
publicitaire	advertising
une publicité télévisée	TV advert
puer	to smell; to stink
puis	then; next
puisque	as; since
un pull	pullover
un pupitre	desk
un pyjama	pyjamas

Q

qu'est-ce que	what
qu'est-ce qu'il y a?	what's the matter?
qu'est-ce que tu as?	what's the matter?
qu'est-ce qui se passe?	what's happening?
un quai	platform; quay
une qualité	quality
quand	when
quand même	even so
une quantité	quantity; amount
quarante	forty
moins le quart	quarter to (time)
et quart	quarter past (time)
un quart	quarter
un quart d'heure	quarter of an hour
un quartier	district; neighbourhood
quatorze	fourteen
quatre	four
quatre-vingt-dix	ninety
quatre-vingts	eighty
quatrième	fourth
que	that; than; what; which
que faire?	what can you do?
québécois	from Quebec
quel	what; what a; which
quel âge as-tu?	how old are you?
quel dommage!	what a pity!
quelle	what; what a; which
quelle heure est-il?	what time is it?
quelqu'un	someone
quelque	some
quelque chose	something
quelque part	somewhere
quelquefois	sometimes
à quelques mètres	a few metres away
une question	question
un questionnaire	questionnaire
une queue	tail; queue
qui	who; that; which
qui est-ce?	who is it?
quinze	fifteen
quinze jours	fortnight
quitter	to leave
quoi	what

■ = masculine noun ■ = feminine noun ■ = verb ■ = adjective

quotidien	daily
quotidienne	daily

R

raconter	to tell
une radio	radio
un radis	radish
une raffinerie	refinery
le rafting	rafting
un ragoût	stew
raide	steep; straight
un raisin	grape
un raisin sec	raisin
une raison	reason
avoir raison	to be right
ramasser	to collect; to pick up
une rame	oar; rowing
à la rame	by rowing
un ramollo	sluggish person
une randonnée	ramble; hike
un rang	row
ranger	to tidy; to put away; to clear up
râpé	grated
râper	to grate
rapide	fast
se rappeler	to remember; to recall
un rapport	report
rapporter	to bring back
se rapporter à	to relate to; to refer to; to connect
une raquette	racquet; bat
rare	rare
rarement	rarely; infrequently
se raser	to have a shave
rassembler	to gather; to collect
un rat	rat
un râteau	rake
rater	to miss; to fail
ravitailler	to refresh; to refuel
rayé	striped
rayer	to cross out
un rayon	department; ray
à rayures	striped
réagir	to react
réaliste	realistic
la réanimation	resuscitation

récent	recent
un récepteur	(telephone) receiver
une réceptionniste	receptionist
un réceptionniste	receptionist
une recette	recipe; receipt
recevoir	to receive; to welcome
la recherche	research
à la recherche de	in search of
tu reçois (*from* recevoir)	you receive
il/elle reçoit (*from* recevoir)	he/she receives
récolter	to collect; to harvest
recommander	to recommend
recommencer	to start again
reconnaître	to recognise
recopier	to copy out; to write out
un record	record
recouvert	covered
une récréation	break
un reçu	receipt
j'ai reçu (*from* recevoir)	I received
recueillir	to collect
reculer	to go back
le recyclage	recycling
une rédaction	editorial staff
redescendre	to come down again
une rediffusion	repeat broadcast
se redresser	to stand up
une réduction	reduction; discount
réduit	reduced
réel	real
réelle	real
refaire	to do again
un réfectoire	canteen
réfléchir	to think; to reflect
un refrain	chorus
refroidir	to go cold
refuser	to refuse; to turn down
regarder	to look at; to watch
un régime	diet
une région	region; area
une règle	ruler
un règlement	rule; regulation
régler	to settle; to sort out
les règles d'or	golden rules
un règne	reign
regretter	to regret; to be sorry

■ = masculine noun ■ = feminine noun ■ = verb ■ = adjective

régulier	regular
régulière	regular
régulièrement	regularly
une reine	queen
rejoindre	to put back together
relancer	to throw again
relaxe	relaxing
relever	to lift
relier	to link; to join up
une religieuse	sort of cream cake
relire	to read again
une reliure	binding
remarquer	to notice; to remark
un remède	remedy
remercier	to thank
remets-toi (*from* se remettre)	get better
remettre	to put back
se remettre	to get better
remonter	to go back up
remplacer	to replace
remplir	to fill; to fill in
remplissez (*from* remplir)	fill in
remuer	to stir; to shake
un renard	fox
une rencontre	meeting
rencontrer	to meet
un rendez-vous	meeting; appointment
se rendre à	to go to
se rendre compte	to realise
rendre visite	to pay a visit
un renne	reindeer
renouveler	to replenish; to renew
rénover	to rebuild
des renseignements	information
la rentrée	back to school
rentrer	to go home
renvoyé	dismissed
réparer	to mend
un repas	meal
repasser	to iron
répéter	to repeat; to rehearse
une répétition	rehearsal
répondre	to reply; to answer
une réponse	answer; reply
un reportage	report; article
se reposer	to rest

■ = masculine noun ■ = feminine noun ■ = verb ■ = adjective

reprendre	to take back
une représentante	representative
un représentant	representative
représenter	to represent
une république	republic
un requin	shark
un réseau	network
une réservation	booking
une réserve	nature reserve
réserver	to reserve; to book
une résidence	residence
résoudre	to solve
respirer	to breathe
ressemblant	similar
ressembler à	to look like
une ressource	resource
un restaurant	restaurant
le reste	rest; remains
rester	to stay; to remain
un résultat	result
un résumé	summary
un retard	delay
en retard	late
retenir	to retain; to keep
un retour	journey home; return
de retour	back again
retourner	to return; to turn over
retraverser	to cross again
un rétroprojecteur	overhead projector
retrouver	to find again
se retrouver	to meet
une réunion	meeting
réussir	to succeed
un rêve	dream
un réveil	alarm-clock
se réveiller	to wake up
révélé	revealed
revenir	to come back
rêver	to dream
rêveur	dreamy
rêveuse	dreamy
au revoir	goodbye
revoir	to see again
une revue	magazine
un rez-de-chaussée	ground floor
au rez-de-chaussée	on the ground floor

le Rhin	(River) Rhine
un rhinocéros	rhinoceros
le rhum	rum
un rhume	cold
ri (*from* rire)	laughed
riche	rich
un rideau	curtain
ridicule	ridiculous
(ne) ... rien	nothing
de rien	don't mention it
rieur	cheerful
rieuse	cheerful
une rigolade	lark; a laugh
rigoler	to laugh; to joke
rigolo	funny
rigolotte	funny
rimer	to rhyme
rire	to laugh
je ris (*from* rire)	I laugh
un risque	risk
il/elle rit (*from* rire)	he/she laughs
une rivière	river
le riz	rice
une robe	dress
un robinet	tap
un robot	robot
un rocher	rock
un roi	king
un rôle	role; part
à tour de rôle	take it in turns
faire du roller	to roller skate
romain	Roman
un roman	novel
un roman policier	detective novel
un roman-photo	picture story
romantique	romantic
un rond	circle
un rond-point	roundabout
une rondelle	slice
ronger	to bite; to gnaw
un ronron	hum; purr
ronronner	to purr
le roquefort	kind of strong cheese
un rosbif	roast beef
rose	pink
rôti	roast

■ = masculine noun ■ = feminine noun ■ = verb ■ = adjective

une roue	wheel
un Rouennais	inhabitant of Rouen
rouge	red
un rouge à lèvres	lipstick
un fauteuil roulant	wheelchair
rouler	to roll; to go
roumain	Romanian
la Roumanie	Romania
rousse	red-haired; ginger
une route	(main) road; route
en route	on the way
une route nationale	an A-road
une gare routière	bus station
roux	red-haired; ginger
le Royaume-Uni	United Kingdom
un ruban	ribbon
une rue	street; road
le rugby	rugby
russe	Russian
la Russie	Russia
rythmé	rhythmic

S

s'il vous plaît	please
sa	his; her; its
le sable	sand
un sac	bag
un sac à dos	back pack; rucksack
un sac de couchage	sleeping bag
un sacco	beanbag
un sachet	bag; small packet
sacré	sacred
sacrifier	to sacrifice
sage	good; well behaved
sain	healthy
je sais (*from* savoir)	I know
une saison	season
il/elle sait (*from* savoir)	he/she knows
une salade	lettuce; salad
un salaire	salary; wage
sale	dirty
salé	savoury; salty
une salle	room
une salle à manger	dining room
une salle d'attente	waiting room
une salle de bains	bathroom
une salle de classe	classroom
une salle de jeux	amusement arcade; games room
une salle de séjour	living room
une salle de sports	sports hall
une salle des professeurs	staffroom
un salon	sitting room; lounge
un salon de coiffure	hairdresser's
une salopette	dungarees
saluer	to greet
salut	hello; goodbye
des salutations	greetings
samedi	Saturday
un sandwich	sandwich
un sanglier	wild boar
sangloter	to sob
sans	without
la santé	health
un sapeur-pompier	fireman

■ = masculine noun ■ = feminine noun ■ = verb ■ = adjective

un sapin	fir tree; Christmas tree
une sardine	sardine
satisfait	satisfied
une sauce	sauce
une saucisse	sausage
un saucisson	sausage (salami type)
sauf	except
un saumon	salmon
un saut	jump
sauter	to jump
sauvage	wild; unsociable
une sauvagerie	wildness
sauver	to save
vous savez (*from* savoir)	you know
savoir	to know
un savon	soap
un schéma	diagram
un schnoque	old man; dodderer
une scie	saw
les sciences	science
scientifique	scientific
un scientifique	scientist
une scientifique	scientist
scier	to saw
scolaire	school
le scoutisme	Scouting and Guiding
se	himself; herself
une séance	performance; session
un raisin sec	raisin
sec	dry
sèche	dry
un sèche-cheveux	hairdryer
sécher	to dry
un séchoir à cheveux	hairdryer
en seconde	in year 11 at school
une seconde	second
secouer	to shake
le secours	first aid
au secours!	help!
un secret	secret
secret	secret
un secrétaire	secretary
une secrétaire	secretary
un secrétariat	school office
secrète	secret
une sécurité	safety

■ = masculine noun ■ = feminine noun ■ = verb ■ = adjective

seize	sixteen
un séjour	stay; living room
le sel	salt
une sélection	selection
une selle	saddle
selon	according to
une semaine	week
sembler	to seem
un sens	meaning; direction
le sens contraire	the other way
un sens unique	one-way street
sensationnel	sensational
sensationnelle	sensational
un sentiment	feeling
sentir	to feel; to smell
se sentir	to feel
séparer	to separate
sept	seven
septembre	September
il sera (*from* être)	it will be
il serait (*from* être)	it would be
une série	series
sérieuse	serious
sérieux	serious
un serpent	snake
serré	tight
se serrer la main	to shake hands
sers-toi (*from* se servir)	help yourself
il/elle sert de (*from* servir)	it's used as
un serveur	waiter
une serveuse	waitress
un service	service; tip
service compris	tip included
une serviette	towel; briefcase
servir	to serve
se servir de	to use
un serviteur	servant
ses	his; her; its
seul	single; only; alone
seulement	only
sévère	strict
des sextuplés	sextuplets
un shampooing	shampoo
le shopping	shopping
un short	shorts
si	if; whether; yes; so

■ = masculine noun ■ = feminine noun ■ = verb ■ = adjective

un siècle	century
une sieste	siesta; afternoon sleep
un signalement	description
un signalisation	signs
un signe	sign
signer	to sign
signifier	to mean
un silence	silence
silencieuse	silent
silencieux	silent
une silhouette	silhouette
simple	single
un singe	monkey
au singulier	in the singular
sinon	if not; unless
un sirop	syrup; cordial
la situation familiale	marital status
situé	situated; located
se situer	to be situated
six	six
sixième	sixth
en sixième	in year 7 at school
le ski nautique	water ski-ing
un slip	knickers; underpants
un slip de bains	swimming trunks
un smoking	dinner jacket
des snickers	trainers
une société	company
une soeur	sister
en soie	made of silk
la soie	silk
avoir soif	to be thirsty
j'ai soif	I'm thirsty
soigner	to treat sick people
(premiers) soins	(first) aid
un soir	evening
une soirée	an evening (of entertainment)
soit ... soit	either ... or
soixante	sixty
soixante-dix	seventy
le sol	ground
solaire	solar
un soldat	soldier
des soldes	sale
le soleil	sun
un coup de soleil	sunstroke

■ = masculine noun ■ = feminine noun ■ = verb ■ = adjective

solitaire	lonely; alone
solonnel	solemn
solonnelle	solemn
une solution	answer
la Somalie	Somalia
sombre	dark
une somme	sum
un sommeil	sleep
avoir sommeil	to be sleepy
nous sommes (*from* être)	we are
un sommet	top
un son	sound
son	his; her; its
un sondage	survey; opinion poll
sonner	to ring
une sonnette	bell
sonore	echoing; ringing
ils/elles sont (*from* être)	they are
une sorcière	witch
je sors (*from* sortir)	I go out
un sort	fate
il/elle sort (*from* sortir)	he/she goes out
une sorte	kind; sort
une sortie	outing; exit
une sortie de secours	emergency exit
sortir	to go out; to take out
soudain	suddenly
soufflé	puffed
souffler	to blow
souffrir	to suffer
souhaiter	to wish
souhaiter la bienvenue	to welcome
se soulever	to raise oneself; to lift oneself
un soulier	shoe
souligner	to underline
une soupe	soup
un souper	supper
un sourcil	eyebrow
sourire	to smile
un sourire	smile
une souris	mouse
sous	under; underneath
sous-marine	underwater
un sous-sol	basement
un sous-titre	subtitle
des sous-vêtements	underwear

■ = masculine noun ■ = feminine noun ■ = verb ■ = adjective

soutenir	to support
souterrain	underground
un soutien-gorge	bra
se souvenir	to remember
un souvenir	souvenir
souvent	often
soyez! (*from* être)	be!
un sparadrap	adhesive plaster
spatial	spatial
un spationaute	astronaut
une spatule	spatula
spécial	special
spécialement	particularly; especially
une spécialité	local dish
un spectacle	performance; show
un spectateur	spectator
la spéléologie	pot-holing
une splendeur	splendour
splendide	magnificent
sponsoriser	to sponsor
un sport	sport
sportif	athletic; sporty
sportive	athletic; sporty
les sports nautiques	water sports
un squelette	skeleton
squelettique	thin as a skeleton
un stade	stadium
un stage	training course
en stage	on a course
une star	(film) star
une station de métro	tube station
une station de ski	ski resort
une station de taxis	taxi rank
une station spatiale	space station
une station-service	petrol station
un stationnement	parking
stationner	to park
une statue	statue
une stéréo	stereo
stéril	sterile
un store	blind
un style	style
un stylo	pen
un succès	success
sucer	to suck
une sucette	lollipop

■ = masculine noun ■ = feminine noun ■ = verb ■ = adjective

le sucre	sugar
sucré	sweet
des sucreries	sweets
sud	south
sud-est	south-east
sud-ouest	south-west
la Suède	Sweden
suédois	Swedish
ça suffit	that's enough
je suis (*from* être)	I am
la Suisse	Switzerland
suisse	Swiss
il/elle suit (*from* suivre)	he/she follows
tout de suite	immediately
une suite	continuation
suivant	following
au suivant!	next (person please)!
suivre	to follow
à suivre	to be continued
un sujet	subject
au sujet de	on the subject of
super	great
une superficie	area
supérieur	upper
un supermarché	supermarket
supplémentaire	extra
supporter	to stand; to bear
sur	on; above; about
sûr	sure; certain
bien sûr	of course; sure!
le surf	surfing
une surface	surface
un surligneur	highlighter
surnaturel	supernatural
une surprise	surprise
surtout	especially; above all
un surveillant	monitor
surveiller	to supervise
un survêtement	tracksuit
un survivant	survivor
survoler	to fly over
en sus	on top; extra
s.v.p. (s'il vous plaît)	please
un sweat	sweatshirt
un sweatshirt	sweatshirt
un symbole	symbol

sympa	nice; friendly
sympathique	nice
un syndicat d'initiative	tourist office
synthétique	man-made
un synthétiseur	synthesiser
un système	system

T

ta	your
un tabac	tobacconist's; tobacco
une table	table
une table de nuit	bedside table
un tableau	blackboard; picture
un tablier	apron
une tâche	task; job
une taille	size
un taille-crayon	pencil sharpener
tais-toi! (*from* se taire)	be quiet!
taisez-vous! (*from* se taire)	be quiet!
un talisman	good-luck object
un tambour	drum
la Tamise	river Thames
tant (de)	so much; so many
tant pis	hard luck; tough!
une tante	aunt
taper	to type; to dial
un tapis	carpet
une tapisserie	tapestry
tard	late
plus tard	later
tarder	to delay
un tarif	price list
une tarte	tart; flan
une tartine	bread and butter
un tas	heap; pile
une tasse	cup
une taupe	mole
Taureau	Taurus
un taux de change	exchange rate
un taxi	taxi
la Tchécoslovaquie	Czechoslovakia
te	you; yourself
un tee-shirt	T-shirt
une télé	telly
télécommandé	remote control
un téléguide	TV guide
un téléphone	telephone
au téléphone	on the (tele)phone
téléphoner	to telephone
un téléspectateur	viewer

■ = masculine noun ■ = feminine noun ■ = verb ■ = adjective

une télévision	television
tellement	so; such
pas tellement	not that much
une température	temperature
une tempête	storm
temporaire	temporary
un temps	weather; time
tout le temps	all the time
à temps	in time
il est grand temps de ...	it's high time to ...
quel temps de chien!	what awful weather!
de temps en temps	from time to time
le temps libre	free time
tenace	stubborn; persistent
tenez (*from tenir*)	here you are; look
tenir	to hold
tenir en laisse	to keep on a lead
un tennis	tennis shoe; tennis
une tentation	temptation
une tenue	outfit
la terminale	year 13 (last year at school)
terminé	finished
(se) terminer	to end
un terrain	pitch; playing area
un terrain de camping	campsite
un terrain de jeux	sports ground
un terrain de tennis	tennis court
un terrarium	enclosure
une terrasse	patio
une terre	earth
par terre	on the ground
terrestre	earthly
tes	your
un testeur	tester
une tête	head
avoir la tête en l'air	to be absent minded
têtu	obstinate
un texte	writing; text
un T.G.V. (Train à Grande Vitesse)	high speed train
un thé	tea
faire du théâtre	to do drama
un théâtre	theatre
un thermomètre	thermometer
un thermos	vacuum flask
un thermostat	thermostat
un thon	tuna fish

un ticket	ticket
tiède	lukewarm; tepid
tiens! (*from tenir*)	look!; here you are!
le tiers monde	Third World
un tigre	tiger
un timbre	stamp
timide	shy
le tir à l'arc	archery
un tirage	circulation (newspapers etc.)
une tirelire	money box
tirer	to pull; to stretch
un tiroir	drawer
un tissu	material
un titre	title
toc toc!	knock knock!
toi	you
à toi	it's your turn
toi-même	yourself
une toile	canvas; cloth
des toilettes	toilets
une toise	height chart
un toit	roof
tolérant	understanding; tolerant
une tomate	tomato
tomber	to fall
tomber en panne	to break down
tomber sur	to come across
ton	your
une tondeuse	lawnmower
tondre	to mow
un tonnerre	thunder
une tortue	tortoise
tôt	early
toucher	to touch
toujours	always; still
faire un tour	to go for a walk round
un tour	tour
une tour	tower
à tour de rôle	in turns
un tourbillon	swirl
le tourisme	tourism
un touriste	tourist
une touriste	tourist
touristique	touristy
tourner	to turn
tourner un film	to shoot a film

■ = masculine noun ■ = feminine noun ■ = verb ■ = adjective

un tournoi	tournament
tous	all; everyone
tous les deux	both
tous les jours	everyday
la Toussaint	All Saint's day
tout	all
en tout	altogether
tout de même	all the same
tout de suite	straight away
tout droit	straight ahead
tout le monde	everybody
tout près	close by
toute	all
de toute façon	anyway
toute la journée	all day
toutes les *x* heures	every *x* hours
tracer	to trace
un tracmots	word search
un tracteur	tractor
en train	by train
un train	train
en train de	in the act of
un train-train	routine
un traîneau	sled
traîner	to hang around
un trait	line
traiter	to call
un trajet	journey
une tranche	slice
tranquille	quiet; peaceful
une tranquillité	peace
transmettre	to pass on
transporter	to carry
un travail	work
travailler	to work
travailleur	hard-working
travailleuse	hard-working
les travaux manuels	handicrafts; CDT
une traversée	crossing
traverser	to cross
treize	thirteen
un tremblement de terre	earthquake
trente	thirty
très	very
un trésor	treasure
une tribune	grandstand

tricher	to cheat
un tricolore	French flag
un tricot	jumper
tricoter	to knit
trilingue	trilingual
un trimestre	(school) term
triste	sad
trois	three
troisième	third
un trombone	trombone; paper clip
une trompe	trunk
se tromper	to make a mistake
une trompette	trumpet
en trompette	turned up
trop (de)	too much; too
une trottinette	child's scooter
un trottoir	pavement
un trou	hole
troublé	worried
un troupeau	flock
une trousse	pencil case
une trousse de bricolage	repair kit
une trousse de secours	first aid kit
une trousse de toilette	toilet bag; sponge bag
trouver	to find
se trouver	to be found; to be situated
un truc	thing; thingy; knack
tu	you
un tube	tube
un tube de dentifrice	tube of toothpaste
tuer	to kill
une tulipe	tulip
la Tunisie	Tunisia
tunisien	Tunisian
tunisienne	Tunisian
un tunnel	tunnel
turc	Turkish
turque	Turkish
la Turquie	Turkey
tutoyer	to use the 'tu' form
un tuyau	pipe
un type	man; bloke
typique	typical

U

ultra	very
un	a; an; one
une	a; an; one
uni	joined; united
un uniforme	uniform
l' Union Soviétique	Soviet Union
unique	only; unique
uniquement	only; exclusively
une unité	unit
un univers	universe
un urbaniste	town planner
usagé	worn; second-hand
un usager	user
une usagère	user
usé	worn out
une usine	factory
un ustensile	utensil; implement
utile	useful
utiliser	to use

■ = masculine noun ■ = feminine noun ■ = verb ■ = adjective

V

il/elle va (*from* aller)	he/she goes
va-t-en!	go away!
des vacances	holiday(s)
en vacances	on holiday
les grandes vacances	summer holidays
des vacanciers	holidaymakers
une vache	cow
vachement	really (slang)
une vague	wave
je vais (*from* aller)	I go
la vaisselle	the dishes; washing up
faire la vaisselle	to do the washing up
le val de Loire	Loire Valley
valable	valid
un valet de coeur	jack of hearts
une valeur	value
une valise	suitcase
une vallée	valley
un vampire	vampire
la vanille	vanilla
une vapeur	steam
une variante	variation
varié	varied
les variétés	TV variety show
Varsovie	Warsaw
tu vas (*from* aller)	you are going
vas-y!	go ahead
un vase	vase
le veau	veal
j'ai vécu (*from* vivre)	I lived
une vedette	(film) star
végétarien	vegetarian
végétarienne	vegetarian
la veille	day before
un vélo	bicycle
en vélo	by bike
un vélo tout terrain (V.T.T.)	mountain bike
un vélomoteur	moped
en velours	made of velvet
un vendeur	shop assistant
une vendeuse	shop assistant
vendre	to sell
vendredi	Friday

■ = masculine noun ■ = feminine noun ■ = verb ■ = adjective

vendu	sold
venez (*from* venir)	come
venir	to come
venir de	to have just
un vent	wind
faire du vent	to be windy
une vente	sale
en vente	for sale
une vente aux enchères	auction
un ventre	stomach
un verbe	verb
vérifier	to check
véritable	absolute; real; true
une vérité	truth
le vermicelle	vermicelli
on verra (*from* voir)	we shall see
un verre	glass
des verres de contact	contact lenses
vers	towards; near; about
un vers	lines (of a song/poem)
Verseau	Aquarius
verser	to pour
en version originale	in the original language
vert	green; ecological
des vertèbres	vertebrae
verticalement	down (in crossword)
avoir le vertige	to suffer from vertigo
une veste	jacket
un vestiaire	cloakroom
un vétérinaire	vet
ils/elles veulent (*from* vouloir)	they want
il/elle veut (*from* vouloir)	he/she wants
veut dire	means
je veux (*from* vouloir)	I want
la viande	meat
une victime	victim
une vidéo	video
une vidéothèque	video hire shop
vider	to empty
un videur	bouncer
une vie	life
vieil	old
vieille	old
je viens (*from* venir)	I come
il/elle vient (*from* venir)	he/she comes
elle vient d'arriver	she has just arrived

Vierge	Virgo
vietnamien	Vietnamese
vietnamienne	Vietnamese
vieux	old
vif	lively
une vigne	vine
une vignette	label; picture
vilain	naughty
une villa	villa
un village	village
une ville	town
en ville	in town
un vin	wine
une vinaigrette	oil and vinegar dressing
vingt	twenty
violet	purple; violet
violette	purple; violet
un violon	violin
un violoncelle	cello
je vis (*from* vivre)	I live
un visage	face
visiter	to visit
un visiteur	visitor
visser	to tighten
il/elle vit (*from* vivre)	he/she lives
vite	fast; quickly
une vitesse	speed; gear
une vitrine	shop window
vivant	alive; lively
vive	lively
vive ... !	long live ...!
vivre	to live
un vocabulaire	vocabulary
voici	here is; here are
une voie	track; platform
voilà	there is; there are
la voile	sailing
une voile	sail
faire de la voile	to go sailing
voir	to see
je vois (*from* voir)	I see
un voisin	neighbour
une voisine	neighbour
il/elle voit (*from* voir)	he/she sees
une voiture	car
en voiture	by car

■ = masculine noun ■ = feminine noun ■ = verb ■ = adjective

une voix	voice
un vol	theft; flight
un volant	steering wheel
voler	to steal; to fly
un voleur	thief
une voleuse	thief
le volley	volleyball
un volontaire	volunteer
vomir	to vomit
ils/elles vont (*from* aller)	they go
vos	your
votre	your
je voudrais (*from* vouloir)	I would like
vous voulez (*from* vouloir)	you want
vouloir	to want; to wish
nous voulons (*from* vouloir)	we want
vous	you
vous-même	yourself
un voyage	journey
voyager	to travel
un voyageur	traveller
un voyant	clairvoyant
une voyelle	vowel
vous voyez (*from* voir)	you can see
voyons (*from* voir)	let's see
un voyou	hooligan; rascal
vrai	true
à vrai dire	to be honest
vraiment	really; truly.
j'ai vu (*from* voir)	I saw/I have seen
une vue	view

W

un **walkman**	personal stereo
les **waters**	toilet
un **week-end**	weekend
un **western**	western (film)

Y

y	there
il y a	there is/ are; ago
un yaourt	yoghurt
des yeux	eyes

Z

un zèbre	zebra
un zéro	nought; zero
un zeste	peel
une zone piétonne	pedestrian precinct
un zoo	zoo
un jardin zoologique	zoo
zut!	damn!; blast!

ENGLISH - FRENCH

A

a	un/une
to be able to (go)	pouvoir (aller)
about	environ; vers
(a book) about (France)	(un livre) sur (la France)
above	au-dessus de; sur
above all	surtout
(to go) abroad	(aller) à l'étranger
absent-minded	distrait
absolutely	absolument
to accept (a cheque)	accepter (un chèque)
accident	un accident
accompanied by	accompagné de
to accompany	accompagner
active	actif/active
activity	une activité
actor	un acteur
actress	une actrice
to add	ajouter
to add up	additionner
address	une adresse
in advance	en avance
advantage	un avantage
adventure	une aventure
adventure film	un film d'aventure
advertisement	une annonce publicitaire
piece of advice	un conseil
(to do) aerobics	(faire de) l'aérobique
aeroplane	un avion
affectionate	affectueux/affectueuse
yours affectionately (at end of a letter)	affectueusement
to be afraid (of)	avoir peur (de)
Africa	l'Afrique
African	africain
after	après

■ = masculine noun ■ = feminine noun ■ = verb ■ = adjective

afternoon	un après-midi
afternoon snack	un goûter
again	encore
against	contre
age	un âge
what is your age?	quel âge as-tu?
aged	âgé
agency	une agence
advertising agency	une agence de publicité
travel agency	une agence de voyages
aggressive	agressif/agressive
agile	agile
(a week) ago	il y a (une semaine)
agreed	d'accord
agricultural	agricole
(first) aid	(premiers) soins
air	l'air
in the open air	en plein air
airbed	un matelas pneumatique
airport	un aéroport
alarm-clock	un réveil
I don't like alcohol	je n'aime pas l'alcool
(an) alcoholic (drink)	(une boisson) alcoolisée
that's all	c'est tout
all	tout (*masculine*); toute (*feminine*); tous (*masculine plural*); toutes (*feminine plural*)
not allowed	interdit
almost	presque
alone	seul; solitaire
already	déjà
alright	d'accord
alsatian dog	un berger allemand
also	aussi
altogether	en tout
always	toujours
I am	je suis (*from* être)
amazing	extraordinaire
ambulance	une ambulance
(in) America	(en) Amérique
American	américain
among	parmi
to amuse	amuser
amusement arcade	une salle de jeux
amusing	amusant

■ = masculine noun ■ = feminine noun ■ = verb ■ = adjective

an	un/une
ancestor	un ancêtre
and	et
angry	furieux/furieuse
to get angry	se fâcher
animal(s)	un animal (des animaux)
ankle	une cheville
to announce	annoncer
announcement	une annonce
to annoy	embêter
annoyed	mécontent
annoying	embêtant
anorak	un anorak
another	encore un(e)
answer	une réponse; une solution
to answer (a question)	répondre (à une question)
an ant	une fourmi
anxious	inquiet/inquiète
any	n'importe quel/quelle
anything	n'importe quoi
anyway	de toute façon
appetite	un appétit
apple	une pomme
apple tree	un pommier
appointment	un rendez-vous
to appreciate	apprécier
appropriate	approprié
approximately	à peu près
apricot	un abricot
(in) April	(en) avril
apron	un tablier
aquarium	un aquarium
Aquarius	Verseau
archery	le tir à l'arc
there are	il y a
they are	ils/elles sont (*from* être)
area	une région
to argue	se disputer
Aries	Bélier
armchair	un fauteuil
army	une armée
around (the house)	autour (de la maison)
to arrest	arrêter
arrival	une arrivée
to arrive	arriver
arrogant	arrogant

■ = masculine noun ■ = feminine noun ■ = verb ■ = adjective

arrow	une flèche
(I like) art	(j'aime) le dessin
art gallery	une galerie d'art
artichoke	un artichaut
article	un article
artist	un artiste/une artiste
as	comme
as (big) as	aussi (grand) que
as well as	ainsi que
Asia	l'Asie
to ask (for)	demander
to ask a question	poser une question
asleep	endormi
to fall asleep	s'endormir
aspirin	une aspirine
athlete	un athlète
athletic	sportif/sportive
(to do) athletics	(faire de) l'athlétisme
Atlantic	atlantique
to attack	attaquer
attic	un grenier
to attract	attirer
aubergine	une aubergine
auburn	châtain (never changes)
August	août
aunt	une tante
Australia	l'Australie
Australian	australien/australienne
Austria	l'Autriche
author	un auteur
autograph	un autographe
automatic	automatique
autumn	l'automne
in autumn	en automne
avenue	une allée; une avenue
average	moyen/moyenne
on average	en moyenne
to avoid	éviter
20 kilometres away	à 20 kilomètres
a few metres away	à quelques mètres
awful	affreux/affreuse; horrible

B

baby	un bébé
back	un dos
in/at the back	en arrière
bad	mauvais
the weather's bad	il fait mauvais
bad-tempered	coléreux/coléreuse
badge	un écusson
badly	mal
badminton	le badminton
bag	un sac
baker	un boulanger/une boulangère
baker's	une boulangerie
balcony	un balcon
ball (large)	un ballon
ball (small)	une balle
ballet	la dance classique
balloon	un ballon
banana	une banane
bank	une banque
bank holiday	un jour férié
bank note	un billet (de banque)
barbecue	un barbecue
barman	un barman
barn	une grange
(in the) basement	(au) sous-sol
basket	un panier
basketball	le basket
basketball player	un basketteur
bass guitar	une basse
bat	une raquette
(to have a) bath	(prendre) un bain
bath tub	une baignoire
bathroom	une salle de bains
battery	une pile
battle	une bataille
bay	une baie
to be	être
beach	une plage
beach umbrella	un parasol
(green) bean	un haricot (vert)

■ = masculine noun ■ = feminine noun ■ = verb ■ = adjective

beard	une barbe
to beat	battre
beautiful	beau/belle
because	parce que
because of	à cause de
to become	devenir
bed	un lit
to go to bed	se coucher
to make the bed	faire le lit
bedroom	une chambre
bedside table	une table de chevet
(roast) beef	(un rôti de) boeuf
beefsteak	un bifteck
been	été (*from* être)
beer	une bière
beetroot	une betterave
before (leaving)	avant (de partir)
to begin (to)	commencer (à)
(at the) beginning (of)	au début (de)
Belgian	belge
Belgium	la Belgique
to believe	croire
bell	une cloche; une sonnette
to belong to	appartenir à; faire partie de
belongings	les affaires
(safety) belt	une ceinture (de sécurité)
bench	un banc
Bermuda shorts	un bermuda
beside	à côté de
besides	d'ailleurs
best	meilleur
best wishes (at end of a letter)	amitiés
(that's) better	(ça va) mieux
to get better	se remettre
get better soon	remets-toi (*from* se remettre) vite
are you better?	ça va mieux?
between	entre
bicycle	une bicyclette; un vélo
bicycle ride	une promenade à vélo
big	grand; gros/grosse
by bike	en vélo
to go for a bike ride	faire du vélo
bike-rider	un cycliste
bilingual	bilingue

■ = masculine noun ■ = feminine noun ■ = verb ■ = adjective

bill	une addition; une note
billion	un milliard
bin	une corbeille; une poubelle
Bingo	le Loto
biology	la biologie
bird	un oiseau
bird watching	l'ornithologie
biro	un bic
birth	une naissance
birthday	un anniversaire
happy birthday	bon anniversaire
biscuit	un biscuit
a bit	un peu
black	noir
blackberry	une mûre
blackboard	un tableau noir
blackcurrant	un cassis
blanket	une couverture
blast!	zut!
blind	aveugle
to block	bloquer
blond	blond
blouse	un chemisier
blue	bleu
to get on board	embarquer
board game	un jeu de société
boarder	un interne/une interne
boarding house	une pension
boarding school	un internat
boat	un bateau
body	un corps
body-building	la musculation
to boil	(faire) bouillir
bold	audacieux/audacieuse
bone	un os
book	un livre
to book (a table)	réserver (une table)
book of stamps	un carnet de timbres
book of tickets (for Paris underground)	un carnet
bookcase	une bibliothèque
booking	une réservation
bookshelf	une étagère
bookshop	une librairie
booth	une cabine
boots	des bottes

■ = masculine noun ■ = feminine noun ■ = verb ■ = adjective

border	une frontière
to bore	ennuyer
to be bored	s'ennuyer
boring	ennuyeux/ennuyeuse
to be born	naître
(I was) born (in)	(je suis) né (à)
to borrow	emprunter
boss	un patron/une patronne
bossy	autoritaire
both	tous les deux
bottle	une bouteille
at the bottom of	en bas de
bow tie	un noeud papillon
bowl	un bol
bowler hat	un chapeau melon
to play bowls	jouer aux boules
box	une boîte
boxing	la boxe
boy	un garçon
boyfriend	un petit ami
brain	un cerveau
brake	un frein
to brake	freiner
brave	courageux/courageuse
some bread	du pain
bread and butter	une tartine
break	une pause; une récréation
to break	casser
to break down	tomber en panne
breakdown	une panne
breakfast	un petit déjeuner
bridge	un pont
briefcase	une serviette
brilliant	génial
to bring	apporter
to bring back	rapporter
British	britannique
Brittany	la Bretagne
brochure	une brochure
broken	cassé
my car has broken down	ma voiture est en panne
brooch	une broche
brother	un frère
brush	une brosse
to brush (your teeth)	se brosser (les dents)
Brussels	Bruxelles

■ = masculine noun ■ = feminine noun ■ = verb ■ = adjective

budgerigar	une perruche
to build	construire
builder	un maçon
building	un bâtiment
built in...	construit en...
bunch (of flowers)	un bouquet (de fleurs)
bunch (of grapes)	une grappe
bunk bed	un lit superposé
to burgle	cambrioler
to burn	brûler
(to catch a) bus	(prendre) un autobus
bus station	une gare routière
businessman	un homme d'affaires
businesswoman	une femme d'affaires
(I am) busy	(je suis) occupé
it's busy	il y a du monde
but	mais
butcher	un boucher/une bouchère
butcher's	une boucherie
butter	le beurre
butterfly	un papillon
button	un bouton
to buy	acheter
by	par

C

cabbage	un chou
cabin	une cabine
café	un café
cage	une cage
cake	un gâteau
cake shop	une pâtisserie
calculator	une calculatrice
to call	appeler
to be called	s'appeler
I am called...	je m'appelle...
what is he called?	comment s'appelle-t-il?
calm	calme
camera	un appareil-photo
to camp	camper
camp bed	un lit de camp
campsite	un camping
can	pouvoir
(a) can (of peaches)	une boîte (de pêches)
I can go	je peux aller
Canada	le Canada
Canadian	canadien/canadienne
candle	une bougie
canoe	un canoë-kayak
(to go) canoeing	(faire) du canoë
canteen	une cantine; un réfectoire
cap	un bonnet; une casquette
captain	un capitaine
car	une voiture
by car	en voiture
car park	un parking
card	une carte
cardigan	un cardigan
to play cards	jouer aux cartes
to be careful	faire attention
careful!	attention!
carefully	attentivement
caretaker	un concierge/une concierge
carnival	un carnival
carpet	un tapis
carrot	une carotte

■ = masculine noun ■ = feminine noun ■ = verb ■ = adjective

to carry	porter
cartoon	un dessin animé
in case of	en cas de
cash-desk	une caisse
cashier	un caissier/une caissière
cassette	une cassette
castle(s)	un château (des châteaux)
casual jacket	un blouson
cat	un chat
to catch	attraper
to catch fire	prendre feu
cathedral	une cathédrale
cauliflower	un chou-fleur
cave	une grotte
C.D.T.	les travaux manuels
to celebrate	fêter
celebration	une fête
cellar	une cave
(I play the) cello	(je joue) du violoncelle
centimeter	un centimètre
central heating	le chauffage central
centre	un centre
century	un siècle
cereal	une céréale
ceremony	une cérémonie
certain	sûr
certainly	décidément
certificate	un brevet
chair	une chaise
champagne	le champagne
champion	un champion/une championne
championship	un championnat
by chance	par hasard
change	la monnaie
I haven't any change	je n'ai pas de monnaie
to change	changer
television channel	une chaîne de télévision
Channel Islands	les îles anglo-normandes
character	un caractère; un personnage
charming	charmant
to chase	chasser
to chat	bavarder
cheap	économique
to cheat	tricher

to check	vérifier
checked	à carreaux
cheek	une joue
cheeky	insolent
cheerful	rieur/rieuse
cheese	un fromage
chemist	un chimiste
chemist's	une pharmacie
chemistry	la chimie
cheque	un chèque
cheque book	un chéquier
cherry	une cerise
(to play) chess	(jouer aux) échecs
chest	une poitrine
chest of drawers	une commode
chestnut brown	châtain (never changes)
(roast) chicken	un poulet (rôti)
chicken cooked in wine	le coq au vin
chief	un chef
child	un enfant/une enfant
I am an only child	je suis fils/fille unique
childhood	une enfance
chimney	une cheminée
China	la Chine
Chinese	chinois
chocolate	un chocolat
drinking chocolate	du chocolat chaud
chocolate bar	une barre chocolatée
choice	un choix
choir	une chorale
to choose	choisir
chop	une côtelette
Christmas	Noël
Christmas Day	le jour de Noël
Christmas tree	un sapin
church	une église
cider	un cidre
cigarette	une cigarette
cinema	un cinéma
circle	un cercle
circus	un cirque
civil servant	un fonctionnaire/une fonctionnaire
clarinet	une clarinette
class	une classe
classical (music)	(la musique) classique

■ = masculine noun ■ = feminine noun ■ = verb ■ = adjective

classroom	une salle de classe
in the classroom	en classe
to clean	nettoyer
(a) clean (glass)	(un verre) propre
cleaning lady	une femme de ménage
to clear the table	débarrasser la table
clever	intelligent
client	un client/une cliente
climate	un climat
to climb	grimper; monter
climbing	l'alpinisme
clock	une horloge; une pendule
to close	fermer
close (by)	tout près
closed	fermé
cloud	un nuage
clumsy	maladroit
coach	un car
by coach	en car
coast	une côte
Coca-Cola	un Coca; un Coca-Cola
cockerel	un coq
cocoa	un cacao
coconut	une noix de coco
coffee	un café
white coffee	un café-crème
coffee with milk	un crème
(a 10 franc) coin	une pièce (de 10 francs)
cold	froid
to be cold	avoir froid
to have a cold	être enrhumé
it's cold	il fait froid
I feel cold	j'ai froid
I've got a cold	j'ai un rhume
to collect	collectionner
collection	une collection
colour	une couleur
column	une colonne
to come	venir
I come	je viens (*from* venir)
to come back	revenir
comfortable	confortable
comic strip	une bande dessinée
company	une compagnie
to compare with	comparer à
comparison	une comparaison

compartment	un compartiment
competition	un concours
competitor	un concurrent/une concurrente
completed	accompli
completely	complètement
complicated	compliqué
composer	un compositeur
comprehensive school	un C.E.S
compulsory	obligatoIre
computer	un ordinateur
computer disk	une disquette
computer programmer	un informaticien/une informaticienne
computer studies; IT	l'informatique
concert	un concert
condition	une condition
confidence	la confiance
confident	confiant
congratulations!	bravo!; félicitations!
train connection	une correspondance
conscientious	consciencieux/ consciencieuse
to consult	consulter
contact lenses	des verres de contact
to contain	contenir
container	un bidon
contents	le contenu
	un continent
to continue	continuer
to contribute	contribuer
convenient	commode
conversation	une conversation
cook	un chef de cuisine; un cuisinier
to cook	cuire; faire la cuisine
cooked cold meat	de la charcuterie
cooker	une cuisinière
(to do the) cooking	(faire la) cuisine
cool	frais/fraîche
to cope	se débrouiller
copy	une copie
to copy	copier
cork (of bottle etc.)	un bouchon
corn	le blé
corner	un coin

correct	juste
corridor	un couloir
Corsica	la Corse
to cost	coûter
costing fifty francs	à cinquante francs
cottage	une chaumière
cotton	le coton; en coton
to count	compter
(shop) counter	un comptoir
(ticket) counter	un guichet
country	un pays
countryside	une campagne
in the countryside	à la campagne
coupon	un bon
of course	bien sûr; naturellement
(main) course	un plat (principal)
court	un court
cousin	un cousin/une cousine
to cover	couvrir
covered	couvert
cow	une vache
craft	l'E.M.T.
crazy	dingue
cream	une crème
sun cream	une crème solaire
to create	créer
credit card	une carte de crédit
crisps	les chips
croissant	un croissant
cross	une croix
to cross	traverser
crossing	une traversée
crossroads	un carrefour
crossword	des mots croisés
cruel	cruel/cruelle
cruise	une croisière
to cry	pleurer
cucumber	un concombre
a cup (of tea)	une tasse (de thé)
cupboard	un placard
curious	curieux/curieuse
curly (hair)	(les cheveux) frisés
currency	la monnaie
curtain	un rideau
cushion	un coussin
customer	un client/une cliente

■ = masculine noun ■ = feminine noun ■ = verb ■ = adjective

to cut (oneself)	(se) couper
cute	mignon/mignonne
cycling	le cyclisme
to go cycling	faire du cyclisme
cycling shorts	un caleçon cycliste

D

D.I.Y.	le bricolage
dad	le papa
daily	quotidien/quotidienne
damage	un dégât
damn!	mince!; zut!
dance	un bal
to dance	danser
dancer	un danseur/une danseuse
dancing	la danse
dangerous	dangereux/dangereuse
dark (blue)	(bleu) foncé
it's dark	il fait nuit
darling	un chéri/une chérie
date	la date
date of birth	la date de naissance
daughter	une fille
day	un jour
all day	toute la journée
every day	tous les jours
next day	le lendemain
per day	par jour
day off	un jour de congé
dead	mort
dead end	un impasse
dear	cher/chère
death	une mort
December	décembre
to decide to	décider de
to declare	déclarer
decorated	décoré
deep	profond
deep freeze	un congélateur
to defend	défendre
definitely	décidément
delicatessen	une charcuterie
delicious	délicieux/délicieuse
to deliver	livrer
demonstration	une manif(estation)
Denmark	le Danemark
dentist	un dentiste
(record) department	un rayon (de disques)

■ = masculine noun ■ = feminine noun ■ = verb ■ = adjective

department store	un grand magasin
departure	un départ
departure gate	une porte
to depend	dépendre
it depends	ça dépend (*from* épendre)
deposit	une caution
depressed	déprimé
to describe	décrire
description	une description
desert	un désert
design and technology	l'E.M.T.
designer	un dessinateur
desk	un bureau; un pupitre
detail	un détail
dialling code	un indicatif
diary	un agenda; un journal
dice	un dé
dictionary	un dictionnaire
(to go on a) diet	(faire) un régime
difference	une différence
different	autre; différent
difficult	difficile
to dine	dîner
dining room	une salle à manger
dinner	un dîner
dinner is served	à table
direct	direct
direction	une direction
director	un directeur/une directrice
dirty	sale
disadvantage	un inconvénient
to disappear	disparaître
disappeared	disparu
disaster	une catastrophe
disco	une boum; une discothèque
to discover	découvrir
discovery	une découverte
to discuss	discuter
to disembark	débarquer
dish-washer	un lave-vaisselle
distant	lointain
in distress	en détresse
to dive	plonger
to divide	diviser

■ = masculine noun ■ = feminine noun ■ = verb ■ = adjective

divorced	divorcé
to do	faire
doctor	un docteur/une doctoresse; un médecin
at/to the doctor's	chez le médecin
doctor's surgery	un cabinet médical
documentary	un documentaire
dog	un chien
doll	une poupée
domino	un domino
donkey	un âne
door	une porte
dormitory	un dortoir
double bass	une contrebasse
Dover	Douvres
downstairs	en bas
dozen	une douzaine (de)
drama	l'art dramatique
to do drama	faire du théâtre
draughts	les dames
to draw	dessiner
drawer	un tiroir
drawing	un dessin
dream	un rêve
to dream	rêver
dress	une robe
I get dressed	je m'habille
dressing room	une cabine d'essayage
to drink	boire
to drive	conduire
driver	un chauffeur; un conducteur
driving licence	un permis de conduire
to drop	laisser tomber
drug	une drogue
dry	sec/sèche
duck	un canard
during	pendant
dustbin	une poubelle
dustman	un éboueur
Dutch	hollandais; néerlandais

E

2 francs each	2 francs la pièce
each (time)	chaque (fois)
ear	une oreille
early	de bonne heure; tôt
to earn	gagner
earring	une boucle d'oreille
earth	une terre
easily	facilement
east	l'est
(at) Easter	(à) Pâques
easy	facile
to eat	manger
the EC (European Community)	la CE
ecology	l'écologie
(on the) edge of	(au) bord (de)
education	un enseignement
effort	un effort
egg	un oeuf
eight	huit
eighteen	dix-huit
eighty	quatre-vingts
either ... or	soit ... soit
elbow	un coude
(my) elder (brother)	(mon frère) aîné
elderly	âgé
electrical appliance	un appareil électrique
electrician	un électricien
elegant	élégant
elephant	un éléphant
eleven	onze
embarrassed	confus
embarrassing	gênant
emergency exit	une sortie de secours
to employ	employer
to empty	vider
to encourage	encourager
end	un bout; une fin
to end	finir; (se) terminer
at the end (of)	au bout (de)
energetic	énergique
energy	une énergie

■ = masculine noun ■ = feminine noun ■ = verb ■ = adjective

engine	un moteur
engineer	un ingénieur
England	l'Angleterre
English	anglais
do you speak English?	parlez-vous anglais?
English Channel	la Manche
Englishman	un Anglais
Englishwoman	une Anglaise
to enjoy oneself	s'amuser
enjoy your meal!	bon appétit!
enjoy your stay!	bon séjour!
enormous	énorme
enough	assez de
that's enough!	ça suffit!
to enter	entrer dans
entertainment	une distraction
enthusiastic	enthousiaste
entrance hall	une entrée
envelope	une enveloppe
equal	égal
equipment	l'équipement
escalator	un escalier mécanique
escape	une évasion
especially	spécialement; surtout
estate	une cité
eurocheque	un eurochèque
European Economic Community	la Communauté Économique Européenne
eurythmics	la gym rythmique et sportive
even	même
evening	un soir
good evening	bonsoir
evening meal	un dîner
every	chaque
every *x* hours	toutes les *x* heures
everybody	tout le monde
everyday	tous les jours
everyone	tout le monde
everywhere	partout
exactly	exactement
to exaggerate	exagérer
example	un exemple
for example	par exemple
except	à part; sauf
exchange	un échange

■ = masculine noun ■ = feminine noun ■ = verb ■ = adjective

to go on an exchange	faire un échange
exchange rate	un cours de change
exciting	passionnant
excuse me	excusez-moi
exercise	un exercice
exercise book	un cahier
an exhibition	une exposition
(emergency) exit	une sortie (de secours)
expensive	cher/chère
experience	une expérience
experiment	une expérience
to explain	expliquer
to explode	exploser
explosion	une explosion
expression	une expression
extra	supplémentaire
to pay extra	payer un supplément
extraordinary	extraordinaire
extrovert	extraverti
eye(s)	un oeil (les yeux)

F

face	un visage
facilities	l'équipement
facing	face à
in fact	en effet; en fait
factory	une usine
to fail (an exam)	rater (un examen)
fair	une fête foraine
it's not fair	ce n'est pas juste
fair hair	les cheveux blonds
faithful	fidèle
to fall	tomber
false	faux/fausse
familiar	familier/familière
family	une famille
famous	célèbre
fan	un passionné/une passionnée
fantastic	fantastique
is it far?	c'est loin?
farm	une ferme
farmer	un fermier/une fermière
fashion	une mode
in fashion	à la mode
fashion show	un défilé de mode
fast	rapide; vite
to fasten	attacher; boucler
fat	gras/grasse; gros/grosse
father	un père
Father Christmas	le père Noël
favourite	favori/favorite; préféré
February	février
I'm fed up	j'ai le cafard; j'en ai marre
to feel ill	avoir mal
felt-tip pen	un feutre
festival	une fête
a few	un peu
fiancé	un fiancé
fiancée	une fiancée
field	un champ
fierce	féroce
fifteen	quinze

■ = masculine noun ■ = feminine noun ■ = verb ■ = adjective

fifth	cinquième
fifty	cinquante
to fight	lutter
file	un dossier
to fill (in a form)	remplir (une fiche)
film	un film
film (for a camera)	une pellicule
film star	une star; une vedette
finally	finalement
to find	trouver
it's fine weather	il fait beau
finger	un doigt
finish	une fin
to finish	finir
fire	un feu; un incendie
fireman	un sapeur-pompier
fireplace	une cheminée
firework (display)	un feu d'artifice
firm	une entreprise
first	premier/première
at first	d'abord
first name	un prénom
fish	un poisson
fisherman	un pêcheur
fishing	la pêche
to go fishing	aller à la pêche
fishing rod	une canne à pêche
fishmonger's	une poissonnerie
fit	en forme
five	cinq
fizzy	gazeux/gazeuse
flag	un drapeau
flan	une tarte
flannel	un gant de toilette
flat	un appartement
flat (tyre)	(un pneu) crevé
block of flats	un immeuble
(what) flavour?	(quel) parfum?
flight	un vol
floor	un plancher
(on the first) floor	(au premier) étage
florist	un fleuriste
flour	une farine
flower	une fleur
(I've got) flu	(j'ai) la grippe
fly	une mouche

■ = masculine noun ■ = feminine noun ■ = verb ■ = adjective

to fly	voler
fog	le brouillard
it's foggy	il fait du brouillard
folder	un dossier
food	la nourriture
food shop	une épicerie
foot	un pied
on foot	à pied
table football	le babyfoot
football	un ballon de foot
football (the game)	le foot/le football
football match	un match de foot
for	pour
for a year	depuis un an
(it is) forbidden to...	(il est) interdit de...
to force to	obliger de
(weather) forecast	la météo
foreign	étranger/étrangère
foreigner	un étranger/une étrangère
forest	une forêt
to forget (to)	oublier (de)
to forgive	pardonner
fork	une fourchette
form	une fiche
on form	en forme
former	ancien/ancienne
fortnight	quinze jours
fortunately	heureusement
forty	quarante
to go forward	avancer
to be found	se trouver
four	quatre
fourteen	quatorze
fourth	quatrième
fox	un renard
fragile	fragile
France	la France
free	gratuit; libre
freeze	geler
it's freezing	il gèle (*from* geler)
French	français
French (the language)	le français
French-speaking	francophone
Frenchman	un Français
Frenchwoman	une Française
fresh	frais/fraîche

■ = masculine noun ■ = feminine noun ■ = verb ■ = adjective

Friday	vendredi
fridge	un frigo
friend (female)	une amie; une copine
friend (male)	un ami; un copain
friendly	sympa
friendship	une amitié
frightening	effrayant
frog	une grenouille
frog's leg	une cuisse de grenouille
from	de
in front of	devant
fruit	un fruit
fruit juice	un jus de fruit
frying pan	une poêle
full	plein
full board	la pension complète
full up	complet/complète
funny	amusant
furniture	des meubles
in (the) future	à l'avenir

G

game	un jeu
games room	une salle de jeux
garage	un garage
garden	un jardin
to do some gardening	faire du jardinage
gas	un gaz
gate	une barrière
gear	une vitesse
Gemini	Gémeaux
general studies	l'éducation civique
generous	généreux/généreuse
genius	un génie
gentle	doux/douce
gentleman	un monsieur
gentlemen	messieurs
gently	doucement
geography	la géographie
gerbil	une gerboise
German	allemand
I'm learning German	j'apprends l'allemand
Germany	l'Allemagne
(in/to) Germany	en Allemagne
to get	chercher
to get in (a car)	monter dans (une voiture)
to get lost	se perdre
to get off (a bus)	descendre (d'un bus)
I get on well (with...)	je m'entends bien (avec...)
to get to know	faire la connaissance de
to get up	se lever
I get up at 7 a.m.	je me lève à 7h.
gherkin	un cornichon
ghost	un fantôme
gift(s)	un cadeau (les cadeaux)
gifted	doué
ginger	roux/rousse
girl	une fille
girlfriend	une petite amie
to give	donner
glass	un verre
glasses	des lunettes
glove	un gant

■ = masculine noun ■ = feminine noun ■ = verb ■ = adjective

to go	aller
I go	je vais (*from* aller)
I go to bed	je vais au lit
they go	ils/elles vont (*from* aller)
to go away	s'en aller
go away!	va-t-en!
to go down (a road)	descendre (une rue)
to go in	entrer dans
go on!	allez!
to go out (of)	sortir (de)
I go out	je sors (*from* sortir)
to go up	monter
goal	un but
goat	une chèvre
God	Dieu
he/she goes	il/elle va (*from* aller)
you are going	tu vas (*from* aller)
gold	l'or
goldfish	un poisson rouge
good	bon/bonne
he's good at maths	il est fort en maths
goodbye	au revoir
goods	des marchandises
goose	une oie
government	un gouvernement
G.P.	un généraliste; un médecin généraliste
gramme	un gramme
grandchildren	les petits-enfants
granddaughter	une petite-fille
grandfather	un grand-père
great grandfather	un arrière grand-père
grandmother	une grand-mère
great grandmother	une arrière grand-mère
grandparents	des grands-parents
grandson	un petit-fils
grape	un raisin
graph	un graphique
grass	l'herbe
greasy	gras/grasse
great	chouette; formidable
Great Britain	la Grande-Bretagne
Greece	la Grèce
greedy	gourmand
Greek	grec/grecque
green	vert

■ = masculine noun ■ = feminine noun ■ = verb ■ = adjective

to greet	saluer
grey	gris
grocer's	une épicerie
on the ground	par terre
(on the) ground floor	(au) rez-de-chaussée
group	un groupe
to grow (vegetables)	cultiver (des légumes)
to guess	deviner
guide	un guide
guidebook	un guide
guinea pig	un cochon d'Inde
I play the guitar	je joue de la guitare
gymnasium	un gymnase
gymnastics	la gymnastique

H

had	eu (*from* avoir)
hair	les cheveux
hairbrush	une brosse à cheveux
hairdresser	un coiffeur/une coiffeuse
hairdresser's	un salon de coiffure
hairdryer	un sèche-cheveux
hairstyle	une coiffure
half	demi
half a kilo	un demi-kilo
half past (telling the time)	et demie
half past midday	midi et demi
half-brother	un demi-frère
half-day	une demi-journée
half-sister	une demi-soeur
ham	un jambon
hamburger	un hamburger
hamster	un hamster
hand	une main
to hand out	distribuer
handicap	un handicap
physically handicapped person	un handicapé physique/ une handicapée physique
handkerchief	un mouchoir
handsome	beau/belle
handwriting	une écriture
to happen	se passer
what's happening?	qu'est-ce qui se passe?
happy	content; heureux/heureuse
hard	dur
hard luck!	tant pis!
hard-working	travailleur/travailleuse
hardware store	une droguerie
he/she has	il/elle a (*from* avoir)
hat	un chapeau
to hate	détester
to have	avoir
I have	j'ai (*from* avoir)
to have to	devoir
I have to leave	je dois partir
you have to (pay)	il faut (payer)
head	une tête

■ = masculine noun ■ = feminine noun ■ = verb ■ = adjective

I've got a headache	j'ai mal à la tête
headlight	un phare
headphones	un casque
heads (on coin)	une face
headteacher	un directeur/une directrice
health	une santé
healthy	sain
to hear	entendre
heart	un coeur
heat	une chaleur
to heat	chauffer
heavy	lourd
hedge	une haie
hedgehog	un hérisson
what height are you?	combien mesures-tu?
helicopter	un hélicoptère
hello	bonjour
hello (on the telephone)	allô
helmet	un casque
to help	aider
help yourself	sers-toi (*from* se servir)
help!	au secours!
hen	une poule
her	son (*masculine*); sa (*feminine*); ses (*plural*)
I see her	je la voie
to her	lui
here	ici
here are	voici
here is	voici
herself	se
to hesitate	hésiter
hi-fi system	une chaîne hi-fi
hidden	caché
to hide	cacher
high	haut
high street	la grand-rue
highway code	un code de la route
to go on a hike	faire une randonnée
hill	une colline
(I hate) him	(je) le (déteste)
to him	lui
himself	se
to hire	louer
his	son (*masculine*); sa (*feminine*); ses (*plural*)

■ = masculine noun ■ = feminine noun ■ = verb ■ = adjective

historic	historique
history	l'histoire
to hit	frapper
hobby	un passe-temps
hockey	le hockey
to hold	tenir
hole	un trou
on holiday	en vacances
holiday(s)	des vacances
summer holidays	les grandes vacances
Holland	les Pays-Bas
at home	à la maison
to go home	rentrer
homework	les devoirs
honest	honnête
honey	un miel
hooligan	un voyou
to hoover	passer l'aspirateur
to hope	espérer
horoscope	un horoscope
horrible	horrible
horror film	un film d'épouvante
horse(s)	un cheval (les chevaux)
(to go) horse riding	(faire de) l'équitation
hospital(s)	un hôpital (les hôpitaux)
hot	chaud
I'm hot	j'ai chaud
it's hot	il fait chaud
hot dog	un hot-dog
hotel	un hôtel
hour	une heure
house	une maison
at my house	chez moi
housewife	une ménagère
(to do) the housework	(faire) le ménage
housing	le logement
hovercraft	un aéroglisseur
how	comment
how are you?	comment ça va?
how many?	combien de?
how much is it?	c'est combien?
how often?	combien de fois?
however	par contre
huge	énorme
hugs and kisses (at end of a letter)	grosses bises

human	humain
hundred	cent
hundreds of...	des centaines de...
to be hungry	avoir faim
to hunt	chasser
(to go) hunting	(aller à) la chasse
in a hurry	pressé
to hurry up	se dépêcher
hurt	blessé
it hurts	ça fait mal
husband	un mari
hut	une cabane
hypermarket	un hypermarché

I

I	je
(vanilla) **ice cream**	une glace (à la vanille)
ice dancing	le patinage artistique
I go **ice skating**	je fais du patin à glace
(good) **idea**	une (bonne) idée
ideal	idéal
identification	une pièce d'identité
to **identify**	identifier
identity card	une carte d'identité
idiot	un imbécile/une imbécile
if	si
ill	malade
illness	une maladie
immediately	immédiatement; tout de suite
impolite	impoli
important	important
impossible	impossible
in	dans
in there	là-dedans
included	compris
India	l'Inde
to **influence**	influencer
information	des renseignements
information office	un bureau de renseignements
ingredient	un ingrédient
inhabitant	un habitant
injection	une piqûre
injured	blessé
inn	une auberge
insect	un insecte
inside	dedans; dans
on the **inside**	à l'intérieur
inspector	un inspecteur
instead of	au lieu de
instruction	une instruction
instructor	un moniteur/une monitrice
musical **instrument**	un instrument de musique
to **interest**	intéresser
interest	un intérêt

■ = masculine noun ■ = feminine noun ■ = verb ■ = adjective

I am interested in	je m'intéresse à
interesting	intéressant
interval	un entracte
interview	une interview
to interview	interviewer
into	dans
to introduce	présenter
investigation	une enquête
invitation	une invitation
to invite	inviter
Ireland	l'Irlande
Irish	irlandais
iron	un fer (à repasser)
to iron	repasser
he/she is	il/elle est (*from* être)
there is	il y a
island	une île
isn't that so?	n'est-ce pas?
I.T.	l'informatique
it is	c'est (*from* être)
Italian	italien/italienne
Italy	l'Italie
item	un article
its	son(*masculine*); sa(*feminine*); ses(*plural*)

J

jacket	une veste
jam	la confiture
January	janvier
javelin	un javelot
jealous	jaloux/jalouse
(pair of) jeans	un jean
Jewish	juif/juive
job	un emploi; un métier
what's his job?	qu'est-ce qu'il fait dans la vie?
to do odd jobs	faire du bricolage
jogging	un footing; un jogging
joke	une blague
to joke	plaisanter
journalist	un journaliste/une journaliste
journey	un voyage
have a good journey!	bon voyage!
judo	le judo
judo club	un club de judo
(fruit) juice	un jus (de fruit)
July	juillet
to jump	sauter
jumper	un tricot
June	juin

K

karate	le karaté
keen	enthousiasmé
to keep	garder
kennel	une niche
key	une clé/une clef
key ring	un porte-clé
keyboard	un clavier
to kill	tuer
kilo	un kilo
kilometre	un kilomètre
kind	gentil/gentille
a kind of	une sorte de
kindness	la gentillesse
king	un roi
(newspaper) kiosk	un kiosque (à journaux)
kiss	une bise
to kiss	(s')embrasser
kitchen	une cuisine
kitten	un chaton
km/h	kilomètre à l'heure
knee(s)	un genou (genoux)
knife/knives	un couteau/couteaux
to knit	tricoter
to knock	frapper
I know	je sais (*from* savoir)
to know (a fact)	savoir
to know (a person)	connaître

L

lab(oratory)	un labo(ratoire)
label	une étiquette
ladder	une échelle
ladies	mesdames
ladies and gentlemen	messieurs-dames
lady	une dame
lake	un lac
lamp	une lampe
to land	atterrir
(foreign) language	une langue (étrangère)
large	grand
last	dernier/dernière
at last	enfin
to last	durer
late	en retard; tard
(he's) late	(il est) en retard
later	plus tard
latest	dernier/dernière
to laugh	rigoler; rire
lawn	un gazon; une pelouse
lazy	paresseux/paresseuse
leaf	une feuille
leaflet	un dépliant
to learn	apprendre
(made of) leather	(en) cuir
to leave	partir
to leave (a car)	laisser (une voiture)
I leave (the house)	je quitte (la maison)
on/to the left	à gauche
left luggage locker	une consigne automatique
left luggage office	une consigne
leg	une jambe
leisure centre	un centre de loisirs
lemon	un citron
lemonade	une limonade
to lend	prêter
length	une longueur
leotard	un body
less	moins
less expensive than	moins cher que
less than (five)	moins de (cinq)
lesson	un cours; une leçon

■ = masculine noun ■ = feminine noun ■ = verb ■ = adjective

to let	laisser
letter	une lettre
lettuce	une laitue; une salade
level	un niveau
Libra	Balance
library	une bibliothèque
lid	un couvercle
life	une vie
lifejacket	un gilet de sauvetage
lift	un ascenseur
to lift	lever
to light	allumer
light	une lumière
light (weight)	léger/légère
to light up	éclairer
lighthouse	un phare
lightning	un éclair
to like	aimer
I would like	je voudrais (*from* vouloir)
like that	comme ça
line	une ligne
lion	un lion
lip	une lèvre
lipstick	un rouge à lèvres
liquid	un liquide
(shopping) list	une liste (des courses)
to listen to (records)	écouter (des disques)
litre	un litre
little	petit
a little	un peu
to live	habiter
I live in Leeds	J'habite à Leeds
lively	animé; vif/vive
living room	une salle de séjour
loaf	un pain
local	local
logical	logique
lollipop	une sucette
London	Londres
lonely	solitaire
long	long/longue
to look after	s'occuper de
to look at	regarder
to look for	chercher
I look like my mother	je ressemble à ma mère
lorry	un camion

■ = masculine noun ■ = feminine noun ■ = verb ■ = adjective

to lose	perdre
I have lost my bag	J'ai perdu mon sac
lost property	des objets trouvés
a lot	beaucoup
out loud	à haute voix
lounge	un salon
to love	adorer
in love	amoureux/amoureuse
love story (film)	un film d'amour
lovely	beau/belle
to lower	baisser
luck	la chance
good luck!	bonne chance!; bon courage!
luckily	heureusement
to be lucky	avoir de la chance
luggage	des bagages
lunch	un déjeuner
to have lunch	déjeuner

M

machine	une machine
mackerel	un maquereau
mad	fou/folle
magazine	un magazine; une revue
magic	magique; la magie
mail	le courrier
main (meal)	(plat) principal
to make	faire
make (of car)	une marque (de voiture)
to make one's mind up to	se décider à
make-up	un maquillage
to put on make-up	se maquiller
man	un homme
to manage	se débrouiller
many	beaucoup de
so many (people)	tant de (gens)
map	une carte
March	mars
a good mark	une bonne note
market	un marché
marmalade	la confiture d'orange
maroon	bordeaux (never changes)
marriage	un mariage
married	marié
to marry	marier
mass (in church)	une messe
(school) master	un maître
masterpiece	un chef d'oeuvre
match	une allumette
mathematics	les mathématiques
maths	les maths
it doesn't matter	ça ne fait rien
May	mai
maybe	peut-être
mayor	un maire
me	moi
meadow	une prairie
meal	un repas
the meal of the day	le plat du jour
what does that mean?	qu'est-ce que cela veut dire?

■ = masculine noun ■ = feminine noun ■ = verb ■ = adjective

meanwhile	entretemps
to measure	mesurer
meat	une viande
mechanic	un mécanicien/une mécanicienne
medal	une médaille
medicine	un médicament
Mediterranean Sea	la Méditerranée
to meet	rencontrer
meeting	un rendez-vous
member	un membre/une membre
member of staff	un employé/une employée
to mend	réparer
don't mention it	de rien; je vous en prie
menu	une carte
(in a) mess	(en) désordre
method	une façon; une méthode
metre	un mètre
microphone	un micro
midday	midi
(in the) middle (of)	(au) milieu (de)
midnight	minuit
mile	un mille
milk	le lait
minced meat	le steak haché
mine	le mien (*masculine*); la mienne (*feminine*); les miens (*masculine plural*); les miennes (*feminine plural*)
mini-skirt	une mini-jupe
mint	la menthe
minus	moins
minute	une minute
mirror	un miroir
Miss	Mademoiselle
to miss	manquer (le train)
mistake	une erreur; une faute
by mistake	par erreur
(school) mistress	une maîtresse
to mix	mélanger
(a) mixed (school)	(une école) mixte
mixed up	mélangé
model	une maquette; un modèle
model-making	le modélisme
modern	moderne

■ = masculine noun ■ = feminine noun ■ = verb ■ = adjective

moment	un instant; un moment
at the moment	pour l'instant
Monday	lundi
money	l'argent
month	un mois
ina bad mood	de mauvaise humeur
in a good mood	de bonne humeur
moon	une lune
moped	une mobylette; un vélomoteur
more	encore; plus
more intelligent than	plus intelligent que
more than twenty	plus de vingt
morning	un matin
most (people)	la plupart (des gens)
mother	une mère
motorbike	une moto
motorcyclist	un motard
motorway	une autoroute
mountain	une montagne
mountain bike	un vélo tout terrain (V.T.T.)
mountain-climber	un alpiniste
(to go) mountaineering	(faire de) l'alpinisme
mouse	une souris
moustache	une moustache
mouth	une bouche
to move	bouger
to move house	déménager
moving house	un déménagement
to mow the lawn	tondre la pelouse
Mr.	Monsieur
Mrs.	Madame
so much	tant (de)
muesli bar	une barre aux céréales
multiplied by	multiplié par
mum	maman
muscle	un muscle
museum	un musée
mushroom	un champignon
music	une musique
musical	une comédie musicale
musician	un musicien/une musicienne
mussel	une moule
must	devoir
I must work	je dois travailler

■ = masculine noun ■ = feminine noun ■ = verb ■ = adjective

mustard	une moutarde
my	mon (*masculine*); ma (*feminine*); mes (*plural*)
myself	me
mystery	un mystère

N

name	un nom
what's your name?	comment t'appelles-tu?
named	nommé
narrow	étroit
nasty	désagréable
national	national
natural	naturel/naturelle
nature	la nature
naughty	méchant
navy blue	bleu marine (*never changes*)
near to	près de
nearby	tout près
nearly	presque
necessary	nécessaire
it is necessary to (leave)	il faut (partir)
neck	un cou
need	un besoin
to need	avoir besoin de
neighbour	un voisin/une voisine
neighbourhood	un quartier
(me) neither	(moi) non plus
nephew	un neveu
nervous	nerveux/nerveuse
net	un filet
Netherlands	les Pays-Bas
never	jamais
new	nouveau/nouvelle
brand new	neuf/neuve
the New Year	le nouvel an
New Zealand	la Nouvelle-Zélande
the news	les actualités
newspaper	un journal
next	puis
(the) next (train)	(le) prochain (train)
next to	à côté de; au bord de
nice	gentil/gentille
it's nice (weather)	il fait beau
niece	une nièce
night	une nuit
good night	bonne nuit

(last) night	(hier) soir
nightclub	une boîte
nightdress	une chemise de nuit
nine	neuf
nineteen	dix-neuf
ninety	quatre-vingt-dix
no	non
no longer	ne ... plus
no more	ne ... plus
nobody	ne ... personne
noise	un bruit
noodles	les nouilles
nor me	moi non plus
normal	normal
normally	généralement; normalement
Normandy	la Normandie
North	le nord
nose	un nez
not	ne ... pas; pas
not at all	pas du tout
not much	pas grand-chose
notebook	un bloc
nothing	ne ... rien
to notice	remarquer
nought	un zéro
(detective) novel	un roman (policier)
November	novembre
now	maintenant
nurse	un infirmier/une infirmière
nut	une noix

O

object	un objet
obstinate	têtu
to obtain	obtenir
October	octobre
(to do) odd jobs	(faire du) bricolage
of	de
(special) offer	une offre (spéciale)
office	un bureau
often	souvent
oil	l'huile
OK	d'accord
old	ancien/ancienne; vieux/ vieille
how old are you?	quel âge as-tu?
omelette	une omelette
on	sur
once	une fois
one	un/une
one-way street	un sens unique
onion	un oignon
only	seulement
only child	un fils unique/une fille unique
open	ouvert
to open	ouvrir
opera (house)	un opéra
operation	une opération
in my opinion	à mon avis
opposite	en face de
or	ou
orange	une orange
orange juice	un jus d'orange
orchestra	un orchestre
order	une commande
out of order	H.S. (hors service)
in order to (go)	pour (aller)
ordinary	ordinaire
to organise	organiser
other	autre; différent
otherwise	autrement

■ = masculine noun ■ = feminine noun ■ = verb ■ = adjective

our	notre (*singular*); nos (*plural*)
outing	une promenade
on the outside (of)	à l'extérieur (de)
(microwave) oven	le four (à micro-ondes)
over there	là-bas
overall	une blouse
it's overcast	il fait gris
overcoat	un manteau
owl	un hibou
to own	posséder
my own room	ma propre chambre
owner	un propriétaire/une propriétaire

■ = masculine noun ■ = feminine noun ■ = verb ■ = adjective

P

to pack a suitcase	faire sa valise
packet (of)	un paquet (de)
page	une page
painter	un peintre/une peintre
painting	une peinture
pair (of)	une paire (de)
palace	un palais
pancake	une crêpe
paper	le papier
parcel	un paquet
parent	un parent
park	un jardin public; un parc
to park	stationner; garer
parking	un stationnement
parrot	un perroquet
part	une partie
(to play a) part	(jouer) un rôle
to be a part of	faire partie de
particular	particulier/particulière
partner	un partenaire/une partenaire
(to have a) party	(avoir) une boum
passage	un passage
passenger	un passager
passport	un passeport
the past	le passé
pasta	les pâtes
pâté	un pâté
patience	une patience
patio	une terrasse
pavement	un trottoir
to pay	payer
to pay a visit	rendre visite
peaceful	paisible; tranquille
peach	une pêche
pear	une poire
peas	des petits pois
pedestrian	un piéton
pedestrian crossing	un passage clouté
pedestrian precinct	une zone piétonne
pen	un stylo

■ = masculine noun ■ = feminine noun ■ = verb ■ = adjective

pencil	un crayon
pencil case	une trousse
pencil sharpener	un taille-crayon
penfriend	un correspondant/une correspondante
penknife	un canif
people	des gens
some people	certains
lots of people	beaucoup de monde
pepper	le poivre
pepper (vegetable)	un poivron
per cent	pour cent
percussion	la batterie
perfect	parfait
performance	une séance
performer	un artiste/une artiste
perfume	un parfum
perhaps	peut-être
permanent	permanent
person	une personne
personal stereo	un walkman
petrol	l'essence
petrol station	une station-service
phone call	un coup de téléphone
photograph	une photo
photography	la photographie
physical education	l'éducation physique; l'E.P.S.
physics	la physique
(I play the) piano	(je joue du) piano
(to have a) picnic	(faire) un pique-nique
picture	une image; un tableau
picturesque	pittoresque
a piece (of)	un morceau (de)
pig	un cochon
pill	un comprimé
pilot	un pilote
pineapple	un ananas
pink	rose
Pisces	Poissons
pitch	un terrain
pitch for a tent	un emplacement
what a pity!	quel dommage!
place	un endroit; un lieu
(a town) plan	un plan (de la ville)
plant	une plante

■ = masculine noun ■ = feminine noun ■ = verb ■ = adjective

plaster	un pansement
(adhesive) plaster	un sparadrap
plastic	plastique
plate	une assiette
platform	un quai; une voie
play	une pièce
to play	jouer
player	un joueur
playground	une cour
pleasant	agréable
please	s'il te (vous) plaît
pleased	content
pleasure	un plaisir
plug	une prise
pocket	une poche
pocket money	l'argent de poche
Poland	la Pologne
police station	un poste de police
police story	un policier
policeman	un agent de police
polite	poli
polluted	pollué
pollution	une pollution
pond	un bassin
poodle	un caniche
pool	le billard américain
poor	pauvre
popular	populaire
pork	le porc
Portuguese	portugais
possibility	une possibilité
possible	possible
post	le courrier
post office	une poste
postcard	une carte postale
poster	une affiche; un poster
postman	un facteur
pot	un pot
potato	une pomme de terre
pound (weight and sterling)	une livre
to pour	verser
practical	pratique
to practise	pratiquer
prawn	une langoustine
to prefer	préférer
to prepare	préparer

present(s)	un cadeau (les cadeaux)
president	un président
press	la presse
pretty	joli
price	un prix
price list	un tarif
priest	un curé
private	privé
prize	un prix
problem	un problème
procession	un défilé
product	un produit
computer program	un programme informatique
to program (computers)	programmer
(TV) programme	une émission
progress	le progrès
proud	fier/fière
PSE	l'éducation civique
pudding	un dessert
to pull	tirer
pullover	un pull
to punch a ticket	composter
puncture	une crevaison
pupil	un élève/une élève
puppy	un chiot
purple	violet/violette
purse	un porte-monnaie
to push	pousser
to put	mettre
to put back	remettre
to put down	poser
to put on	mettre
I put on (a coat)	je mets (un manteau)
pyjamas	un pyjama

■ = masculine noun ■ = feminine noun ■ = verb ■ = adjective

Q

quality	une qualité
quantity	une quantité
quarrel	une dispute
quarter	un quart
quarter of an hour	un quart d'heure
quarter past (time)	et quart
quarter to (time)	moins le quart
queen	une reine
question	une question
queue	une queue
to queue up	faire la queue
quickly	vite
be quiet	tais-toi!/taisez-vous! (*from* se taire)
quiet	tranquille
quite	assez

R

rabbit	un lapin
racquet	une raquette
radio	une radio
radish	un radis
railway	un chemin de fer
(in the) rain	(sous la) pluie
to rain	pleuvoir
rainbow	un arc-en-ciel
raincoat	un imperméable
it's raining	il pleut (*from* pleuvoir)
raisin	un raisin sec
rare	rare
rarely	rarement
raspberry	une framboise
rat	un rat
rather	plutôt
to read	lire
(I like) reading	(j'aime) la lecture
ready	prêt
real	authentique; réel/réelle
really	vraiment
receipt	un reçu
recent	récent
receptionist	un réceptionniste; une réceptionniste
recipe	une recette
to recognise	reconnaître
to recommend	recommander
record	un disque
to record	enregistrer
record player	un électrophone
recorder	une flûte à bec
recording	un enregistrement
red	rouge
red-haired	roux/rousse
reduced	réduit
reduction	une réduction
to refuse to	refuser de
register	un appel; un cahier d'appel

■ = masculine noun ■ = feminine noun ■ = verb ■ = adjective

registration number	un numéro d'immatriculation
regular	régulier/régulière
regularly	régulièrement
rehearsal	une répétition
relative	un parent
relaxed	décontracté
relaxing	relaxe
religious education	l'instruction religieuse
to remain	rester
to remember	se rappeler; se souvenir de
to rent	louer
to replace	remplacer
to reply	répondre
(school) report	un bulletin (scolaire)
representative	un représentant/une représentante
to reserve	réserver
to rest	se reposer
restaurant	un restaurant
result	un résultat
to return	retourner
rice	le riz
rich	riche
to go for a ride	faire une promenade en auto
ridiculous	ridicule
on/to the right	à droite
to be right	avoir raison
right-handed	droitier/droitière
right?	n'est-ce pas?
ring	une bague
to ring	sonner
to ring up	appeler; téléphoner à
risk	un risque
river	une rivière
Riviera	la Côte d'Azur
road	une rue
roast	rôti
rock	un rocher
rocket	une fusée
to roller skate	faire du roller
roller skates	des patins à roulettes
roller skating	le patin à roulettes
romantic	romantique

roof	un toit
room	une pièce; une salle
rough book	un cahier de brouillon
roughly	à peu près
roundabout	un rond-point
route	un itinéraire
rubber	une gomme
(made of) rubber	(en) caoutchouc
rubbish	les déchets
rucksack	un sac à dos
rude	impoli
rugby	le rugby
ruler	une règle
to run	courir
runner	un coureur
to rush	se précipiter

S

sad	triste
safety	une sécurité
safety belt	une ceinture de sécurité
to go sailing	faire de la voile
sailor	un marin
salad	une salade
salad cream	une mayonnaise
sale	des soldes
for sale	en vente
salmon	un saumon
salt	le sel
same	même
sand	le sable
sandcastle	un château de sable
sandwich	un sandwich
sardine	une sardine
Saturday	samedi
sauce	une sauce
saucepan	une casserole
sausage	une saucisse
sausage (salami type)	un saucisson
to save	sauver
to save up	faire des économies
to say	dire
scarf	une écharpe; un foulard
school	une école; un collège
night school	une école du soir
nursery school	une école maternelle
primary school	une école primaire
school bag	un cartable
school office	un secrétariat
school party	un groupe scolaire
schoolboy	un écolier
schoolgirl	une écolière
science	les sciences
scientific	scientifique
scientist	un scientifique/une scientifique
scissors	des ciseaux
to score (a goal)	marquer (un but)
Scotland	l'Écosse

■ = masculine noun ■ = feminine noun ■ = verb ■ = adjective

Scots	écossais
Scouting and Guiding	le scoutisme
sea	une mer
by the sea	au bord de la mer
seafood	des fruits de mer
seasickness	un mal de mer
season	une saison
an (empty) seat	une place (libre)
seated	assis
second	deuxième; une seconde
second-hand	d'occasion
secondary school	un collège; un C.E.S.
secret	un secret; secret/secrète
secretary	un secrétaire/une secrétaire
to see	voir
I see	je vois (*from* voir)
you can see	vous voyez (*from* voir)
to seem	sembler
selfish	égoïste
to sell	vendre
to send	envoyer
sentence	une phrase
to separate	séparer
Septembre	septembre
serial	un feuilleton
series	une série
serious	grave; sérieux/sérieuse
to serve	servir
service	le service
to set the table	mettre la table
the sun sets	le soleil se couche
settee	un canapé
seven	sept
seventeen	dix-sept
seventy	soixante-dix
several	plusieurs
to sew	coudre
sewing	la couture
shadow	une ombre
to shake hands	se serrer la main
shampoo	un shampooing
shape	une forme
to share	partager
to have a shave	se raser
she	elle

■ = masculine noun ■ = feminine noun ■ = verb ■ = adjective

sheep	un mouton
sheet of paper	une feuille
shelf	une étagère
shelter	un abri
to shine	briller
shirt	une chemise
shock	un choc
shocking	choquant
shoe	une chaussure; un soulier
what shoe size?	quelle pointure?
shop	une boutique; un magasin
shop assistant	un vendeur/une vendeuse
shop keeper	un commerçant
shop window	une vitrine
to go shopping	faire des courses
to do some shopping	faire des achats
shopping centre	un centre commercial
short	court
shorts	un short
shoulder	une épaule
to shout	crier
show	un spectacle
to show	montrer
(to have) a shower	(prendre) une douche
Shrove Tuesday	Mardi gras
to shut	fermer
shy	timide
sick	malade
I feel sick	j'ai mal au coeur
sick bay	une infirmerie
side	un côté
sideboard	un buffet
sight	une curiosité; un monument
sign	un panneau; un signe
to sign	signer
silence	un silence
silent	silencieux/silencieuse
silver	l'argent
similar	pareil/pareille
since (the war)	depuis (la guerre)
to sing	chanter
singer	un chanteur/une chanteuse
single	seul

■ = masculine noun ■ = feminine noun ■ = verb ■ = adjective

a single ticket	un billet simple
kitchen sink	un évier
Sir	Monsieur
sister	une soeur
to sit	s'installer
to sit down	s'asseoir
sit down!	assieds-toi/asseyez-vous! (*from* s'asseoir)
sitting down	assis
sitting room	un salon
situated	situé
six	six
sixteen	seize
sixth	sixième
sixth form college	un lycée
sixty	soixante
(what) size?	(quelle) taille?
to skate	patiner
skateboard	une planche à roulettes
(to go) skating	(faire du) patinage
ice skating	le patin à glace
skating rink	une patinoire
ski resort	une station de ski
skin	une peau
skirt	une jupe
sky	un ciel
to sleep	dormir
sleeping bag	un sac de couchage
sleepy	endormi
slice	une tranche
colour slide	une diapositive
slim	mince
to slim	maigrir
to slip	glisser
slippers	des chaussons
slow	lent
slowly	lentement
small	petit
smart	chic (*never changes*)
smell	une odeur
to smile	sourire
smile	un sourire
to smoke	fumer
smoker	un fumeur/une fumeuse
non smoking	non fumeur/non fumeuse
snack	un casse-croûte

snackbar	un buffet
snail	un escargot
snake	un serpent
snow	la neige
it's snowing	il neige
snowman	un bonhomme de neige
so	alors; donc; si
so big	si grand
so-so	comme ci comme ça
soap	le savon
(TV) soap	un feuilleton
social studies	l'instruction civique
sock	une chaussette
sofa	un canapé
soft	doux/douce
soldier	un soldat
some	du (*masculine*); de la (*feminine*); des (*plural*)
someone (else)	quelqu'un (d'autre)
something	quelque chose
sometimes	quelquefois
somewhere	quelque part
somewhere else	ailleurs
son	un fils
song	une chanson
soon	bientôt
see you soon!	à bientôt!
to be sorry	regretter
(I am) sorry	(je suis) désolé
a sort of	une sorte de
sound	un son
soup	un potage; une soupe
(in the) south (of)	(dans le) sud (de)
south-east	le sud-est
south-west	le sud-ouest
souvenir	un souvenir
space	un espace
spade	une bêche
(in/to) Spain	(en) Espagne
Spanish	espagnol
to speak	parler
special	spécial
(I wear) spectacles	(je porte) des lunettes
spectator	un spectateur
speed	une vitesse

■ = masculine noun ■ = feminine noun ■ = verb ■ = adjective

how do you spell that?	çela s'écrit comment? (*from* s'écrire)
to spend (a week)	passer (une semaine)
to spend (money)	dépenser (de l'argent)
spider	une araignée
spinach	des épinards
to sponsor	sponsoriser
sponsorship	le patronage
spoon	une cuillère
dessert spoon	une cuillère à soupe
spoonful	une cuillerée
sport	un sport
sporting event	un événement sportif
sports association/club	une association sportive
sports centre	un centre sportif
sports ground	un terrain de jeux
sports hall	une salle de sports
sports jersey	un maillot
sporty	sportif/sportive
spot	un bouton
(in) spring	(au) printemps
square	carré
(town) square	une place
stadium	un stade
staff	un personnel
staffroom	une salle des professeurs
stair	une marche
(flight of) stairs	un escalier
stamp	un timbre
to stamp	composter
stamp collecting	la philatélie
I can't stand that	j'ai horreur de ça
standing (up)	debout
star	une étoile
to start	commencer
starter (food)	une entrée
stately home(s)	un château (des châteaux)
(bus) station	une gare (routière)
stationer's	une papeterie
statue	une statue
stay	un séjour
to stay (at home)	rester (à la maison)
to steal	voler
step	une marche
step-brother	un demi-frère
step-father	un beau-père

■ = masculine noun ■ = feminine noun ■ = verb ■ = adjective

step-mother	une belle-mère
step-sister	une demi-soeur
stereo	une chaîne stéréo; une stéréo
stick	une canne
to stick	coller
sticker	un autocollant
still	encore; toujours
sting	une piqûre
stomach	un estomac; un ventre
I've got stomach ache	j'ai mal au ventre
stone	une pierre
bus stop	un arrêt d'autobus
to stop	s'arrêter (de)
storey	un étage
storm	un orage; une tempête
story	une histoire
straight	droit; raide
straight ahead	tout droit
straight away	tout de suite
straight on	tout droit
straightaway	aussitôt
strange	bizarre
stranger	un étranger/une étrangère
strawberry	une fraise
street	une rue
strict	sévère
(on) strike	(en) grève
striped	rayé
to stroke	caresser
to go for a stroll	faire une balade
strong	fort
stubborn	obstiné; tenace
student	un étudiant/une étudiante
to study	étudier
stupid	bête
style	un style
subject	un sujet
school subject	une matière
suburb	une banlieue
in the suburbs	en banlieue
subway	un passage souterrain
to succeed (in)	réussir (à)
success	un succès
suddenly	soudain
sugar	le sucre

■ = masculine noun ■ = feminine noun ■ = verb ■ = adjective

suit	un costume
suitable	approprié
suitcase	une valise
to pack a suitcase	faire sa valise
sum	un calcul
(in) summer	(en) été
summer holidays	les grandes vacances
sun	le soleil
sun cream	le lait solaire
to sunbathe	bronzer
sunbathing	le bronzage
sunburn	un coup de soleil
Sunday	dimanche
sunglasses	des lunettes de soleil
its sunny	il fait du soleil
sunny period	une éclaircie
sunshade	un parasol
supermarket	un supermarché
supper	un souper
sure	sûr
surface	une surface
surname	le nom de famille
surprise	une surprise
to be surprised	s'étonner
surrounded by	entouré de
surrounding area	des environs
survey	une enquête; un sondage
to swap	échanger
sweatshirt	un sweat/un sweatshirt
Sweden	la Suède
to sweep	balayer
sweet	un bonbon; doux/douce
sweet shop	une confiserie
to swim	nager
to have a swim	se baigner
(to go) swimming	(faire de) la natation
swimming costume	un maillot de bain
swimming pool	une piscine
indoor swimming pool	une piscine couverte
swing	une balançoire
Swiss	suisse
to switch on	allumer
Switzerland	la Suisse

T

table	une table
(to play) table tennis	(jouer au) ping-pong
tablecloth	une nappe
tablet	un comprimé
tails (on coin)	pile
to take	prendre
to take (a test)	passer (un examen)
to take (somebody somewhere)	emmener
to take away (food)	à emporter
to take off (clothes)	enlever (des vêtements)
to take part in	participer à
to take place	avoir lieu
I'll take that!	je prends ça!
take-off (of an aeroplane)	un décollage
to talk	parler
talkative	bavard
tall	grand
tanned	bronzé
tap	un robinet
to tap dance	faire des claquettes
tape	une bande
tape recorder	un magnétophone
taste	un goût
to taste	déguster; goûter
Taurus	Taureau
taxi	un taxi
tea	un thé
teacher	un professeur
team	une équipe
teddy bear	un nounours
teenager	un adolescent/une adolescente
telephone	un téléphone
on the telephone	au téléphone
to telephone	téléphoner (à)
telephone kiosk	une cabine téléphonique
television	une télévision
to tell	dire; raconter
telly	une télé

temperature	une température
to have a temperature	avoir de la fièvre
ten	dix
tennis	le tennis
tennis court	un terrain de tennis
tennis shoes	des tennis
(school) term	un trimestre
terrible	affreux/affreuse
test	un contrôle; une interro(gation)
river Thames	la Tamise
to thank	remercier
thank you	merci
thanks to	grâce à
that	ça; que
that's all right	ça va
the	le (*masculine*); la (*feminine*); les (*plural*)
theatre	un théâtre
their	leur (*singular*)/leurs (*plural*)
theme park	un parc d'attractions
then	puis
there	là
there are	il y a
there is	il y a
therefore	donc
thermometer	un thermomètre
these	ces
they	ils (*masculine*)/elles (*feminine*)
thief	un voleur/une voleuse
thigh	une cuisse
thin	maigre
thing	une chose
thingy	un machin; un truc
to think (about)	penser (de)
to think (of)	penser (à)
third	troisième
I'm thirsty	J'ai soif
thirteen	treize
thirty	trente
this is	c'est (*from* être)
this way	par ici
thousand	mille
thousands of	des milliers de

to threaten	menacer
three	trois
throat	une gorge
through	par
to throw	jeter; lancer
thumb	un pouce
thunder	un tonnerre
Thursday	jeudi
ticket	un billet
return ticket	un aller-retour
single ticket	un aller simple
ticket collector	un contrôleur
ticket office	un guichet
ticket-punch	un composteur
tidy	en ordre
to tidy	ranger
tie	une cravate
pair of tights	un collant
till	une caisse
time	le temps
at the same time	à la fois
long time	longtemps
all the time	tout le temps
in time	à temps
from time to time	de temps en temps
free time	le temps libre
what time is it?	quelle heure est-il?
three times	trois fois
timetable	un horaire
school timetable	un emploi du temps
tin	une boîte
tin-opener	un ouvre-boîtes
tiny	minuscule
tip	un pourboire
tip included	service compris
tired	fatigué
tiredness	la fatigue
tiring	fatigant
toast	le pain grillé
tobacco	du tabac
tobaconnist's	un tabac
today	aujourd'hui
together	ensemble
toilets	les toilettes
tomato	une tomate
tomorrow	demain

too	aussi
too (much)	trop de
tooth	une dent
toothbrush	une brosse à dents
toothpaste	un dentifrice
torch	une lampe de poche
tortoise	une tortue
to touch	toucher
tour	un tour
tourism	le tourisme
tourist	un touriste/une touriste
tourist office	un syndicat d'initiative
towards	vers
towel	une serviette
tower	une tour
town	une ville
in town	en ville
(in the) town centre	(au) centre-ville
town hall	un hôtel de ville
toy	un jouet
track	une piste
railway track	une voie
tracksuit	un survêtement
tractor	un tracteur
traffic	la circulation
traffic jam	un embouteillage
traffic lights	des feux
train	un train
by train	en train
to train	s'entraîner
trainer	un entraîneur
trainers	des baskets
training	un entraînement
to travel	voyager
traveller	un voyageur
traveller's cheque	un chèque de voyage
tray	un plateau
treasure	un trésor
(family) tree	un arbre (généalogique)
trip	une excursion
trolley	un chariot
trombone	un trombone
trophy	une coupe
trousers	un pantalon
true	vrai
(to play the) trumpet	(jouer de la) trompette

trunks	un maillot de bain
truth	une vérité
to try to	essayer de
T-shirt	un tee-shirt
tube (of toothpaste)	un tube (de dentifrice)
tube station	une station de métro
Tuesday	mardi
tulip	une tulipe
tuna fish	un thon
tunnel	un tunnel
Turkey	la Turquie
to turn	tourner
TV set	un poste de TV
twelve	douze
twenty	vingt
twin	un jumeau/une jumelle
two	deux
two-wheeler	un deux-roues
type	un genre
to type	taper
typical	typique
(a flat) tyre	un pneu (crevé)

U

ugly	laid
umbrella	un parapluie
unbearable	insupportable
unbelievable	incroyable
uncle	un oncle
under	sous
underground	souterrain
underground railway	un métro
underneath	sous
to understand	comprendre
have you understood?	tu as compris? (*from* comprendre)
unemployed	au chômage
unfortunately	malheureusement
unhappy	malheureux/malheureuse
uniform	un uniforme
United Kingdom	le Royaume-Uni
United States	les États-Unis
unknown	inconnu
unpleasant	désagréable
until	jusqu'à
upstairs	en haut
us	nous
to use	employer; utiliser
useful	utile
useless	débile; nul/nulle
he's useless at maths	il est nul en maths
usual	normal
usually	en général; d'habitude

V

vacant	libre
to vacuum	passer l'aspirateur
vacuum cleaner	un aspirateur
vacuum flask	un thermos
valley	une vallée
van	une camionnette
vanilla	la vanille
various	divers
vase	un vase
veal	le veau
vegetable	un légume
vegetarian	végétarien/végétarienne
versus	contre
very	très
very much	beaucoup
vet	un vétérinaire
vicious	méchant
video	une vidéo
video cassette	une cassette-vidéo
video hire shop	une vidéothèque
video recorder	un magnétoscope
view	une vue
villa	une villa
village	un village
(I play the) violin	(je joue du) violon
Virgo	Vierge
to visit	visiter
visitor	un visiteur
voice	une voix
volleyball	le volley

■ = masculine noun ■ = feminine noun ■ = verb ■ = adjective

W

waffle	une gaufre
wage	un salaire
to wait (for)	attendre
waiter	un garçon; un serveur
waiting room	une salle d'attente
waitress	une serveuse
to wake up	se réveiller
(in/to) Wales	(au) Pays de Galles
walk	une promenade
to walk	marcher
to go for a walk	faire une promenade
to walk the dog	promener le chien
walkman	un baladeur
wall	un mur
wallet	un portefeuille
to want	désirer; vouloir
I want	je veux (*from* vouloir)
you want	vous voulez (*from* vouloir)
war	une guerre
warder	un gardien
wardrobe	une armoire
it's warm	il fait chaud
I was	j'étais (*from* être)
to wash	laver
washbasin	un lavabo
to get washed	se laver
(to do the) washing	(faire la) lessive
washing facilities	un bloc sanitaire
washing machine	une machine à laver
(to do the) washing up	(faire la) vaisselle
wasp	une guêpe
watch	une montre
to watch (television)	regarder (la télévision)
watch out!	attention!
water	une eau
fresh water	eau douce
water ski-ing	le ski nautique
water sports	des sports nautiques
waterfall	une cascade
to wave	faire bonjour
way	un chemin
on the way	en route

■ = masculine noun ■ = feminine noun ■ = verb ■ = adjective

that way	par là
we	nous
weak	faible
to wear	porter
weather	un temps
weather forecast	une météo
the weather is poor	il fait mauvais
what awful weather!	quel temps de chien!
wedding	un mariage
Wednesday	mercredi
week	une semaine
per week	par semaine
weekend	un week-end
to weigh	peser
weight	un poids
welcome	un accueil
welcome!	bienvenue à vous!
well	bien
Welsh	gallois
I went	je suis allé (*from* aller)
west	l'ouest
West Indian	antillais
West Indies	les Antilles
western (film)	un western
what	qu'est-ce que; quoi
what can you do?	que faire?
what is...like?	comment est...?
what's happening?	qu'est-ce qui se passe?
what's the matter?	qu'est-ce qu'il y a?
wheat	le blé
wheel	une roue
wheelchair	un fauteuil roulant
when	quand
where	où
whether	si
which	quel (*masculine singular*); quelle (*feminine singular*); quels (*masculine plural*); quelles (*feminine plural*)
white	blanc/blanche
Whitsun	la Pentecôte
who (is it)?	qui (est-ce)?
whole	entier/entière
why	pourquoi
wide	large
wife	une femme

■ = masculine noun ■ = feminine noun ■ = verb ■ = adjective

wild	sauvage
wildlife	la faune
to win	gagner
wind	un vent
window	une fenêtre
(to go) windsurfing	(faire de) la planche à voile
it's windy	il fait du vent
wine	un vin
winner	un gagnant
(in) winter	(en) hiver
to wipe	essuyer
to wish	vouloir
to wish for	désirer
with	avec
without	sans
woman	une femme
to wonder	se demander
wood	un bois
made of wood	en bois
(made of) wool	(en) laine
word	un mot
word processor	une machine à traitement de textes
word search	un tracmots
in other words	c'est-à-dire
work	un travail
to work	travailler
to work out	calculer
worker	un ouvrier/une ouvrière
worksheet	une fiche
world	un monde
worn out	usé
worried	anxieux/anxieuse
don't worry	ne t'inquiète pas
wrapping	un emballage
wrestling	le catch
wretched	misérable
to write	écrire
to be written	s'écrire
wrong	faux/fausse; mauvais

Y

year	un an/une année
school year	une année scolaire
in year 7 at school	en sixième
I'm in year 8	je suis en cinquième
year tutor	un conseiller d'éducation
yellow	jaune
yes	oui
yesterday	hier
you	vous; te; toi; tu
young	jeune
your	ton (*masculine*); ta (*feminine*); tes (*plural*); votre (*singular*); vos (*plural*)
yours (at end of a letter)	amicalement
yourself	te; toi-même; vous-même
youth centre	une maison des jeunes
youth club	un club des jeunes
youth hostel	une auberge de jeunesse

Z

zero	un zéro
zoo	un zoo; un jardin zoologique

CHECK LIST

LES NOMBRES		NUMBERS
un (une)	1	one
deux	2	two
trois	3	three
quatre	4	four
cinq	5	five
six	6	six
sept	7	seven
huit	8	eight
neuf	9	nine
dix	10	ten
onze	11	eleven
douze	12	twelve
treize	13	thirteen
quatorze	14	fourteen
quinze	15	fifteen
seize	16	sixteen
dix-sept	17	seventeen
dix-huit	18	eighteen
dix-neuf	19	nineteen
vingt	20	twenty
vingt et un (une)	21	twenty-one
vingt-deux	22	twenty-two
trente	30	thirty
quarante	40	fourty
cinquante	50	fifty
soixante	60	sixty
soixante-dix	70	seventy
soixante et onze	71	seventy one
soixante-douze	72	seventy-two
quatre-vingts	80	eighty
quatre-vingt-un (une)	81	eighty-one
quatre-vingt-dix	90	ninety
quatre-vingt-onze	91	ninety-one
cent	100	a hundred
cent un (une)	101	a hundred and one
trois cents	300	three hundred
trois cent un (une)	301	three hundred and one
mille	1 000	a thousand
un million	1 000 000	a million

NOMBRES ORDINAUX	ORDINAL NUMBERS
premier (première) 1 er	first, 1st
deuxième, 2e or 2ème	second, 2nd
troisième, 3e or 3ème	third, 3rd
quatrième	fourth, 4th
cinquième	fifth, 5th
sixième	sixth, 6th
septième	seventh
huitième	eighth
neuvième	ninth
dixième	tenth

LES FRACTIONS etc	FRACTIONS etc
un demi	a half
un tiers	a third
deux tiers	two thirds
un quart	a quarter
un cinquième	a fifth
zéro virgule cinq, 0.5	(nought) point five, 0.5
trois virgule quatre, 3.4	three point four, 3.4
dix pour cent	ten per cent
cent pour cent	a hundred per cent

LES JOURS	DAYS OF THE WEEK
lundi	Monday
mardi	Tuesday
mercredi	Wednesday
jeudi	Thursday
vendredi	Friday
samedi	Saturday
dimanche	Sunday
Quel jour sommes-nous?	What day is it?

LES MOIS	MONTHS OF THE YEAR
janvier	January
février	February
mars	March
avril	April
mai	May
juin	June
juillet	July
août	August
septembre	September
octobre	October
novembre	November
décembre	December
Quelle est la date?	What's the date?

■ = masculine noun ■ = feminine noun ■ = verb ■ = adjective

LES SAISONS	SEASONS
le printemps	Spring
l'été	Summer
l'automne	Autumn
l'hiver	Winter
au printemps	In the Spring
en été	In the Summer
en automne	In the Autumn
en hiver	In the Winter

1994 = mil neuf cent quatre-vingt-quatorze
or dix-neuf cent quatre-vingt-quatorze

TELLING THE TIME

Quelle heure est-il?	What time is it?

The hours

Il est une heure	1 o'clock
Il est deux heures	2 o'clock etc

Minutes past the hour

Il est trois heures cinq	3.05 (five past three)
Il est trois heures dix	3.10 etc

Minutes to the hour

Il est quatre heures moins cinq	3.55 (five to four)
Il est quatre heures moins dix	3.50 (ten to four)

Quarter and half hours

Il est trois heures et quart	3.15 (a quarter past three)
Il est trois heures et demie	3.30 (half past three)
Il est quatre heures moins le quart	3.45 (quarter to four)

Midday and midnight

Il est midi	12 noon
Il est minuit	12 midnight
Il est midi cinq	12.05 pm
Il est midi et demi	12.30 pm

24 hour clock

Il est treize heures	13.00
Il est quatorze heures cinq	14.05
Il est quinze heures quinze	15.15
Il est seize heures trente	16.30
Il est dix-sept heures quarante-cinq	17.45

VERBS

-er verbs
je mang***e***
tu mang***es***
il/elle mang***e***
nous mange***ons***
vous mang***ez***
ils/elles mang***ent***

-ir verbs
je fin***is***
tu fin***is***
il/elle fin***it***
nous fin***issons***
vous fin***issez***
ils/elles fin***issent***

-re verbs
je vend***s***
tu vend***s***
il/elle vend
nous vend***ons***
vous vend***ez***
ils/elles vend***ent***

être - to be
je suis
tu es
il/elle est
nous sommes
vous êtes
ils/elles sont

avoir - to have
j'ai
tu as
il/elle a
nous avons
vous avez
ils/elles ont

aller - to go
je vais
tu vas
il/elle va
nous allons
vous allez
ils/elles vont